D1486798

THE RAINTREE
ILLUSTRATED
SCIENCE
ENCYCLOPEDIA

VOLUME 12

ORG-POI

RAINTREE
STECK-VAUGHN
L I B R A R Y
A Division of Steck-Vaughn Company

Managing Editors

Corinn Codye
Writer and editor of social science
  and science textbooks
Paul Q. Fuqua
Writer and editor of films, filmstrips,
  and books on scientific subjects

Raintree Editorial

Barbara J. Behm, Editor
Elizabeth Kaplan, Editor
Lynn M. Marcinkowski, Project Editor
Judith Smart, Editor-in-Chief

Raintree Art/Production

Suzanne Beck, Art Director
Kathleen A. Hartnett, Designer
Carole Kramer, Designer
Eileen Rickey, Typesetter
Andrew Rupniewski, Production Manager

USING THE RAINTREE ILLUSTRATED SCIENCE ENCYCLOPEDIA

You are living in a world in which science, technology, and nature are very important. You see something about science almost every day. It might be on television, in the newspaper, in a book at school, or some other place. Often, you want more information about what you see. *The Raintree Illustrated Science Encyclopedia* will help you find what you want to know. The Raintree encyclopedia has information on many science subjects. You may want to find out about mathematics, biology, agriculture, the environment, computers, or space exploration, for example. They are all in *The Raintree Illustrated Science Encyclopedia*. There are many, many other subjects covered as well.

There are eighteen volumes in the encyclopedia. The articles, which are called entries, are in alphabetical order through the first seventeen volumes. On the spine of each volume, below the volume number, are some letters. The letters above the line are the first three letters of the first entry in that volume. The letters below the line are the first three letters of the last entry in that volume. In Volume 1, for example, you see that the first entry begins with **aar** and that the last entry begins with **art**. Using the letters makes it easy to find the volume you need.

In Volume 18, there are interesting projects that you can do on your own. The projects are fun to do, and they illustrate important science principles. Also in Volume 18, there are two special features—an index and a bibliography.

Main Entries. The titles of the main entries in *The Raintree Illustrated Science Encyclopedia* are printed in capital letters. They look like this: **CAMERA**. At the beginning of most entries, you will see a phonetic pronunciation of the entry title. In the front of each volume, there is a pronunciation key. Use it the same way you use your dictionary's pronunciation key.

At the end of each entry, there are two sets of initials. They often look like this: P.Q.F./J.E.P. The first set belongs to the person or persons who wrote the entry. The second set belongs to the special consultant or consultants who checked the entry for accuracy. Pages iii and iv in Volume 1 give you the names of all these people.

Cross-References. Sometimes, a subject has two names. The Raintree encyclopedia usually puts the information under the more common name. However, in case you look up the less common name, there will be a cross-reference to tell you where to find the information. Suppose you wanted to look up something about the metric temperature scale. This scale is usually called the Celsius Scale. Sometimes, however, it is called the Centigrade Scale. The Raintree encyclopedia has the entry **CELSIUS SCALE**. If you looked up Centigrade Scale, you would find this: **CENTIGRADE SCALE** *See* CELSIUS SCALE. This kind of cross-reference tells you where to find the information you need.

There is another kind of cross-reference in the Raintree encyclopedia. It looks like this: *See* CLOUD. Or it looks like this: *See also* ELECTRICITY. These cross-references tell you where to find other helpful information on the subject you are reading about.

Projects. At the beginning of some entries, you will see this symbol: **PROJECT** It tells you that there is a project related to that entry in Volume 18.

Illustrations. There are thousands of photographs, graphs, diagrams, and tables in the Raintree encyclopedia. They will help you better understand the entries you read. Captions describe the illustrations. Many of the illustrations also have labels that point out important parts.

Index. The index lists every main entry by volume and page number. Many subjects that are not main entries are also listed in the index.

Bibliography. In Volume 18, there is also a bibliography for students. The books in this list are on a variety of topics and can supplement what you have learned in the Raintree encyclopedia.

The Raintree Illustrated Science Encyclopedia was designed especially for you, the young reader. It is a source of knowledge for the world of science, technology, and nature. Enjoy it.

PRONUNCIATION KEY

Each symbol has the same sound as the darker letters in the sample words.

ə	balloon, ago	i	rip, ill	sh	shoot, machine
ər	learn, further	ī	side, sky	t	to, stand
a	map, have	j	join, germ	th	thin, death
ā	day, made	k	king, ask	t̪h	then, this
ä	father, car	l	let, cool	ü	pool, lose
aů	now, loud	m	man, same	ů	put, book
b	ball, rib	n	no, turn	v	view, give
ch	choose, nature	ng	bring, long	w	wood, glowing
d	did, add	ō	cone, know	y	yes, year
e	bell, get	ȯ	all, saw	z	zero, raise
ē	sweet, easy	ȯi	boy, boil	zh	leisure, vision
f	fan, soft	p	part, scrap	'	strong accent
g	good, big	r	root, tire	'	weak accent
h	hurt, ahead	s	so, press		

GUIDE TO MEASUREMENT ABBREVIATIONS

All measurements in *The Raintree Illustrated Science Encyclopedia* are given in both the customary, or English, system and the metric system [in brackets like these]. Following are the abbreviations used for various units of measure.

Customary Units of Measure

mi. = miles	cu. yd. = cubic yards
m.p.h. = miles per hour	cu. ft. = cubic feet
yd. = yards	cu. in. = cubic inches
ft. = feet	gal. = gallons
in. = inches	pt. = pints
sq. mi. = square miles	qt. = quarts
sq. yd. = square yards	lb. = pounds
sq. ft. = square feet	oz. = ounces
sq. in. = square inches	fl. oz. = fluid ounces
cu. mi. = cubic miles	°F. = degrees Fahrenheit

Metric Units of Measure

km = kilometers	cu. km = cubic kilometers
kph = kilometers per hour	cu. m = cubic meters
m = meters	cu. cm = cubic centimeters
cm = centimeters	ml = milliliters
mm = millimeters	kg = kilograms
sq. km = square kilometers	g = grams
sq. m = square meters	mg = milligrams
sq. cm = square centimeters	°C = degrees Celsius

For information on how to convert customary measurements to metric measurements, see the **METRIC SYSTEM** article in Volume 10.

ORGANISM (ȯr′gə niz′əm) *Organism* is a general term for any particular form of life. Organisms are usually classified as belonging to one of five groups called kingdoms. Two of these kingdoms are the animal kingdom and the plant kingdom. All organisms consist of one or many cells. Viruses, which do not consist of cells, are on the borderline between living and nonliving matter. *See also* CLASSIFICATION OF LIVING ORGANISMS; LIFE; VIRUS.

W.R.P./C.R.N.

ORIOLE (ȯr′ē ōl′) The orioles are perching birds that belong to genus *Icterus* in the American blackbird family, Icteridae. The males are usually black and yellow or black and red with white spots. They are known for their warbled songs. The females are usually not as brightly colored and sing simpler songs. Orioles eat insects, sometimes prying them out of trees with their beaks. Most orioles live in warm, wooded areas. The northern oriole (*Icterus galbula*) is common in the United States. The eastern and western forms of this species differ in color. In Europe and Asia, the name *oriole* is given to birds that belong to an entirely different family, the Oriolidae. *See also* BIRD; BLACKBIRD; PERCHING BIRD.

A.J.C./L.L.S.

ORNITHOLOGY (ȯr′nə thäl′ə jē) Ornithology is the biological science that studies birds. It deals with all matters involving birds' lives, distribution, classification, and history. Ornithologists, the scientists who study birds, research the activities of birds, which include mating, nesting, care of young, feeding, and migration. (*See* BIRD; MIGRATION.)

People have been interested in birds since prehistoric times. Most of the early writings on birds were brief descriptions of or stories about birds. In the Middle Ages, people were interested in training birds for hunting. In the eighteenth and nineteenth centuries, scientists described and classified most known species of birds. In the late nineteenth and the twentieth centuries, many ornithologists concentrated on the anatomy (body structure) and behavior of birds as well as their relationship to other organisms and their environment.

An ornithologist puts a band on a bird. The bird will then be set free and observed.

Much information about the distribution and activities of birds has come from a technique known as banding. In banding, a small metal or plastic band is attached to the leg of a captured bird. The bird is then set free. Amateur bird watchers throughout the world are able to supply scientists with information about the banded birds. In fact, ornithology is one of the few sciences that relies heavily on the observations of amateurs. Birds were first banded in the nineteenth century. Now, hundreds of thousands of birds are banded every year.   A.J.C./L.L.S.

OSCILLATION (äs'ə lā'shən) Oscillation is the type of movement made, for example, by a pendulum. (*See* PENDULUM.) Suppose that a pendulum is held to one side and then let go. It swings to the vertical (up-and-down) position and then moves through that position until gravity stops it on the other side. (*See* GRAVITY.) The pendulum then returns through the vertical position and stops when it reaches the point at which it was released. This is called a single oscillation. The time taken for a single oscillation is called the period of oscillation. The number of single oscillations in a second is called the frequency of oscillation. (*See* FREQUENCY.) Another example of an oscillation is the movement of a guitar string when it is plucked. The string moves back and forth through the position it has when it is at rest. All

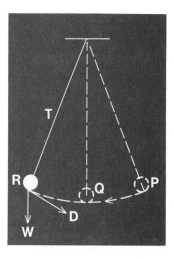

When set in motion, the bob weight of a simple pendulum (right) oscillates along an arc RQP. As it reaches the R end of the arc, the pull of gravity stops it. Tension of thread T gives downward pull (W) a sideways effect (D), so the bob moves back to Q. As it does so, it gathers speed. The bob slows again at the P end of the arc, and the oscillation cycle begins again.

oscillations eventually die away. For example, as the pendulum swings, its maximum position from the vertical position becomes smaller. This is called damping. It is caused by a number of different effects. The most impor-

tant is the effect of gravity on the pendulum. The friction of the air also has an effect. *See also* FRICTION.   M.E./J.T.

OSCILLATOR (äs'ə lāt'ər) Oscillators are electronic devices that changed direct electrical current into a signal of desired frequency. A direct current is a flow of electric charges in one direction. Frequency is the number of vibrations per second. (*See* DIRECT CURRENT.)

An oscillator is actually a kind of amplifier. It strengthens a current and then feeds part of the amplified current back into itself to change it into a specific frequency. (*See* AMPLIFIER.) Oscillators are used in radio and telephone receivers and in other equipment. *See also* ELECTRICITY.   M.E./L.L.R.

OSCILLOSCOPE (ä sil'ə skōp') An oscilloscope is an electronic instrument. It is used to show the oscillation (vibration) of an electric signal. (*See* OSCILLATION.) An oscilloscope contains a cathode-ray tube similar to the tube found in television sets. (*See* CATHODE-RAY TUBE.) The screen of the cathode-ray tube displays the oscillation as wavy lines or other patterns.

As in all cathode-ray tubes, a beam of electrons is directed at the fluorescent screen and appears as a spot of light. As the beam is made to move from left to right, the electrical signal to be studied is fed into the oscilloscope. The beam then moves up and down in correspondence with the oscillations of the signal. The movements of the beam trace a pattern on the screen.

Oscilloscopes are used by engineers to test electronics equipment. They are also used by doctors to study electrical activity of the brain and heart. An oscilloscope can be used to show any kind of vibration, such as sound waves. In this case, a device called a transducer is needed. It changes the sound waves into electric signals. *See also* ELECTRONICS; SOUND; TRANSDUCER.   M.E./L.L.R.

OSMIUM *See* ELEMENT.

OSMOSIS (äz mō′səs) Osmosis is a special kind of diffusion. (*See* DIFFUSION.) Osmosis is the movement of a liquid, usually water, through a semipermeable membrane from one solution into another solution. A semipermeable membrane is a sheet or layer that that allows some, but not all, substances to pass through it. A solution is a mixture of a liquid (solvent) and dissolved particles (solute). (*See* SOLUTION AND SOLUBILITY.) In osmosis, the movement of a solvent is usually from a dilute solution (low concentration of solute) into a stronger solution (high concentration of solute). As a result, the stronger solution becomes more dilute. The rate of osmosis depends on the difference in the strengths of the solutions. The greater the difference, the faster the rate of osmosis. Osmosis continues until both solutions are in equilibrium, or of equal strength.

The membranes of a living cell are semipermeable. (*See* CELL; MEMBRANE.) Plants absorb water and dissolved minerals from the soil by osmosis. Osmosis is then used to move the water and dissolved minerals through the plant, cell by cell. Osmosis also maintains turgor pressure. Turgor pressure is the pressure of water in the cell. It gives the cell form and strength. When there is a decrease in turgor pressure, the plant will seem wilted: it will not have its regular stiffness. Turgor pressure changes are responsible for some types of plant movement. (*See* MOVEMENT OF PLANTS.)

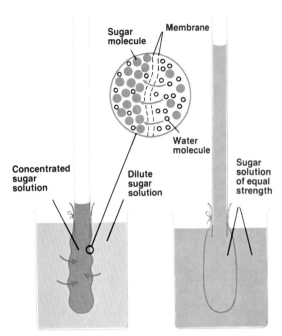

A bag of concentrated sugar solution (above left) is tied to the end of a glass tube and immersed in a dilute sugar solution. The bag (a semipermeable membrane) allows only water to pass through it. Water molecules (inset) pass into the bag. As the solution in the bag becomes more dilute, osmotic pressure forces the liquid up the tube (above right).

In the human body, osmosis allows the transfer of water and dissolved nutrients from the blood into the cells. It also helps remove wastes and excess water from the cells. (*See* HOMEOSTASIS.) Osmosis is also important in the removal of wastes and excess water from the blood by the kidneys. (*See* KIDNEY.)

A type of reverse osmosis can be caused by adding pressure to the system. Normally, in a system made up of solutions of seawater (salt water) and fresh water separated by a semipermeable membrane, osmosis would cause the water to move from the fresh water into the seawater in an attempt to reach equilibrium. When pressure is applied to the seawater, however, the water moves out of that solution and into the fresh water. This process is sometimes used for emergency purification of seawater for drinking purposes.

A.J.C./M.J.C.; M.H.M.; C.R.N.

OSPREY (äs′prē) The osprey is a bird of prey that belongs to the hawk family, Accipitridae. (*See* HAWK.) It is often called the fish hawk. It may grow to lengths of 22 in. [55 cm] and may have a wingspan of 54 in. [135 cm]. The wings and back of the osprey are brown. The underside of the body and the head are white. The bird has a dark band running across its eyes that looks like a mask.

Ospreys usually eat only fish. They dive into the water from heights as high as 150 ft. [45 m]. Unlike the bald eagle and most other fish-eating birds of prey, ospreys will plunge completely underwater to catch a fish. Although they are not very numerous, ospreys are found all over the world, including in most coastal and lake areas of North America.

The Long Island Sound area in the northeastern United States was at one time the largest North American breeding ground for ospreys. In the late 1960s, the birds almost disappeared from the area because of water pollution. Pesticides and other chemicals in the water had poisoned the fish that the birds ate. (*See* PESTICIDE; POLLUTION.) Chemicals from the poisoned fish collected in the ospreys' bodies and caused their eggshells to be very thin. Most of the eggshells broke before the eggs were ready to hatch. In the 1970s, ornithologists (scientists who study birds) began to bring healthy eggs from other areas to the nests on Long Island Sound. The eggs were hatched by new parents. Today, there is less poisoning of the waters, and ospreys are becoming more numerous. S.R.G./L.L.S.

OSTRICH (äs′trich) The ostrich is the world's tallest bird. There is only one living species of ostrich (*Struthio camelus*). It grows to heights of 8 ft. [2.4 m]. It cannot fly, but it can run very fast. The wings and tail of the ostrich are

white. The body of the male is black. The body of the female is brown. The feathers of the ostrich are unlike those of most birds. They resemble the fluffy down of young birds.

The ostrich is a flightless bird that lives in the grasslands and deserts of Africa and the Arabian Peninsula. It is the world's tallest bird.

Ostriches live in the grasslands and deserts of Africa and the Arabian Peninsula. They were once very common. However, many were killed for their feathers. Today, large flocks are seen only in a few parts of eastern and southern Africa. *See also* BIRD. S.R.G./L.L.S.

OTTER (ät′ər) The otter, a carnivorous mammal, is a member of the weasel family, Mustelidae. (*See* CARNIVORE; MAMMAL; WEASEL.) Otters live close to water and spend most of their time in it. They are expert swimmers and divers, and they can stay underwater for three or four minutes. Otters move awkwardly on land.

Otters live on every continent except Australia. Most otters weigh from 10 to 30 lb. [4.5

The otter is a water-loving member of the weasel family. It makes its home in burrows or under rocky ledges. In some areas, otters have been hunted to extinction for their fur.

out. Webbing between the toes helps the otter swim swiftly. Otters have two layers of brownish gray fur. Long, coarse outer hairs, called guard hairs, protect their short, thick underfur. The underfur traps air and keeps the otter's skin dry. Otters live alone, except at breeding time. They eat crayfish, crabs, and various fish. They also eat clams, frogs, insects, snails, snakes, and, occasionally, water birds.

Otters usually live in burrows (holes) in riverbanks or under rocky ledges. Young otters do not swim until they are seven months old. W.R.P./J.J.M.

to 14 kg] and grow 3 to 4.5 ft. [0.9 to 1.4 m] in length, including the tail. The giant otter of South America can grow 7 ft. [2 m] long.

An otter has a small, flattened head; a long, thick neck; and a thick tail that narrows to a point. Special muscles enable the otter to tightly close its ears and nostrils to keep water

OVARY (ōv′rē) An ovary is a reproductive structure. In animals, the ovary produces ova (eggs) in the female. It also makes sex hormones that affect the body shape of females, their reproductive function, and pregnancy. (*See* EGG; HORMONE; REPRODUCTION.) In flowering plants, the ovary is an enlarged area at the base of the pistil that produces ovules. The ovules contain eggs. *See also* FLOWER; OVULE.
C.M./J.J.F.; M.H.M.

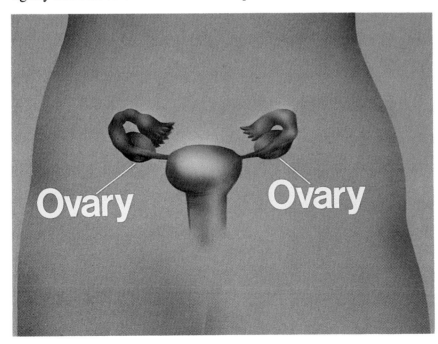

The eggs of female animals are produced in the ovaries. The ovaries also produce hormones. Pictured at left are human ovaries.

OVULE (äv′ yül) An ovule is that part of most plants' reproductive organs that contains the female gamete, or egg. After the egg is fertilized by a pollen grain, which contains the male gamete, the ovule matures into a seed.

The ovule is unprotected in gymnosperms. The ovules lie on the scales of structures called cones. In angiosperms, the ovules are protected by female reproductive structures called ovaries, which are part of the pistil. *See also* ANGIOSPERM; EGG; FERTILIZATION; GYMNOSPERM; OVARY; PLANT KINGDOM; REPRODUCTION.

P.Q.F./J.E.P.

OWL (aůl) An owl is a bird of prey that belongs to the order Strigiformes. It has a large head and eyes, short neck, broad wings, and sharp talons, or claws. About 130 species of owls are found around the world. Eighteen species live in North America. Owls vary in size. The largest North American owl is the

This illustration shows an owl, its talons outstretched, swooping down on a mouse. Most owls hunt for food at night.

great gray owl. It grows 22 in. [55 cm] long and has a wingspan of 60 in. [150 cm]. The elf owl is the smallest owl in North America. It grows only 5.25 in. [13.3 cm] long and has a wingspan of 15 in. [37.5 cm].

Most owls are active at night. (*See* NOCTURNAL HABIT.) They have excellent eyesight and hearing, which help them find and catch food. Their main food consists of rodents and other small mammals. During the night, owls fly quietly about, searching for food. During the day, they sit in trees and old buildings. The call of many owls is an eerie "who." *See also* BIRD.

S.R.G./L.L.S.

OXALIC ACID (äk sal′ik as′əd) Oxalic acid, $(COOH)_2 \cdot 2H_2O$, is a weak organic (carbon-containing) acid. It occurs as clear, colorless crystals. It is very poisonous and can cause paralysis of the nervous system. (*See* ACID; CRYSTAL.) Oxalic acid is found in some mushrooms. Salts of oxalic acid are called oxalates. They are also poisonous. They are found in several plants, including rhubarb, dock, and wood sorrel. (*See* SALTS.)

Oxalic acid is used in industry to make inks and dyes and to bleach materials. It is also used to make polishes for metals. Plants are not used as a source of oxalic acid in industry. Rather, oxalic acid is manufactured by heating a substance called sodium formate, which changes into sodium oxalate. Sulfuric acid is then added to obtain oxalic acid. *See also* SULFURIC ACID.

M.E./A.D.

OXIDATION AND REDUCTION Oxidation (äk′sə dā′shən) and reduction (ri dək′-shən) are two very important processes in chemical reactions. (*See* CHEMICAL REACTION.) The atoms of all elements contain smaller particles called electrons. (*See* ATOM; ELECTRON; ELEMENT.) When an element combines with another element, its atoms gain or lose electrons. Because an electron has a negative electric charge, the atoms of an element that gain an electron also gain a negative charge. When this happens, the element is said to have an oxidation number of –1. If the atoms each gain two electrons, the oxidation number of the element becomes –2. In the same way, if the atoms each lose an electron, they gain a positive charge. The element's oxidation number is then +1. An element on its own has an oxidation number of 0. If the oxidation number of an element increases, it is said to be oxidized. If it decreases, it is reduced. For example, calcium and oxygen combine to form calcium oxide. When this happens, the calcium atoms each lose two electrons to the oxygen atoms. Therefore, the oxidation number of the calcium increases from 0 to +2. It has been oxidized. The oxidation number of the oxygen changes from 0 to –2. It has been reduced.

The most common form of oxidation is when oxygen is added to an element or compound. (*See* COMPOUND.) That is why the process is called oxidation. However, other elements besides oxygen can oxidize substances. For example, sodium combines with chlorine to form sodium chloride. The chlorine oxidizes the sodium because it gains electrons from chlorine. In the same way, the sodium reduces the chlorine.

Substances that can oxidize other substances are called oxidizing agents. Many of them contain large amounts of oxygen in their molecules. (*See* MOLECULE.) Examples of oxidizing agents include oxygen (O_2), ozone (O_3), hydrogen peroxide (H_2O_2), and nitric acid (HNO_3). Other oxidizing agents, such as chlorine and fluorine, do not contain oxygen.

Substances that reduce other substances are called reducing agents. Hydrogen and carbon are common reducing agents. *See also* OXYGEN.   M.E./A.D.

OXIDE (äk′sīd) Oxides are compounds that contain oxygen and one other element. Such compounds include water, which is hydrogen oxide (H_2O); quartz, which is silicon dioxide (SiO_2); and quicklime, which is calcium oxide (CaO). Many minerals consist of oxides. For example, the most important mineral source of aluminum is bauxite, which is aluminum oxide (Al_2O_3). (*See* COMPOUND; ELEMENT; MINERAL; OXYGEN.)

Some oxides, such as sulfur dioxide (SO_2), dissolve in water to form acids. (*See* ACID.) They are called acidic oxides and are usually the oxides of nonmetals. Other oxides are called basic oxides. Some of these, such as sodium oxide (Na_2O), dissolve in water to form hydroxides. (*See* BASE.) Basic oxides combine with acids to form salts. This is called neutralization. (*See* NEUTRALIZATION; SALTS.) Basic oxides are oxides of metals. Some oxides are both acidic and basic. They form salts with both acids and bases. They are called amphoteric oxides. Zinc oxide (ZnO) is an amphoteric oxide.   M.E./A.D.

OXYACETYLENE TORCH (äk′ sē ə set′-əl ən tôrch) An oxyacetylene torch is a very hot torch used for welding and cutting metals. (*See* METAL AND METALLURGY; WELDING AND CUTTING.) Mixtures of oxygen and acetylene are used in oxyacetylene torches. Acetylene gas burns in oxygen to produce a very hot flame. (*See* ACETYLENE.) The flame has a temperature of about 6,332°F. [3,500°C]. In welding, the heat of the flame melts two pieces of metal that are to be joined. The molten (melted) metals mix together and are then allowed to cool and become solid.

An oxyacetylene torch used for welding has two main parts: a nozzle and a blowpipe. Acetylene and oxygen are kept separately, usually in two cylinders. The gases enter the blowpipe separately through two valves. They are mixed together and then leave the nozzle. The mixture is ignited (set on fire) as it leaves the nozzle. Different proportions of oxygen and acetylene are used for different metals.

For cutting metal, a slightly different kind of torch is used. The flame heats the metal but does not heat it enough to make it melt. A blast of high-pressure oxygen is passed through the center of the flame and directed at a certain point on the metal. The metal oxidizes away. (*See* OXIDATION AND REDUCTION.) The torch is slowly moved over the surface of the metal, cutting as it goes.

The flame produced when acetylene burns is very bright. For this reason, oxyacetylene mixtures are sometimes used for lighting, such as in miners' lamps.
M.E./J.M.

OXYGEN (äk′si jən) Oxygen is an element that, at room temperature, is a colorless, odorless gas. (*See* ELEMENT; GAS.) Oxygen is one of the gases in the air. It makes up about 21 percent of the air. (*See* AIR.)

Oxygen was discovered by two chemists working independently of each other. Karl Scheele, a Swedish chemist, discovered oxygen in about 1772. Then Joseph Priestley, an English chemist, discovered oxygen in 1774. (*See* PRIESTLEY, JOSEPH; SCHEELE, KARL WILHELM.)

Oxygen is important to almost every form of life. People and land animals take in air and extract oxygen from it in their lungs. The oxygen then enters the blood and travels around the body. Water animals use the oxygen that is dissolved in the water. They have structures called gills to obtain the oxygen. Plants absorb

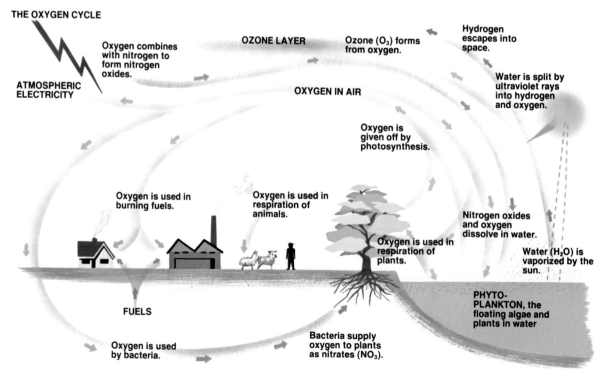

THE OXYGEN CYCLE

ATMOSPHERIC ELECTRICITY

Oxygen combines with nitrogen to form nitrogen oxides.

OZONE LAYER

Ozone (O_3) forms from oxygen.

Hydrogen escapes into space.

Water is split by ultraviolet rays into hydrogen and oxygen.

OXYGEN IN AIR

Oxygen is given off by photosynthesis.

Oxygen is used in burning fuels.

Oxygen is used in respiration of animals.

Nitrogen oxides and oxygen dissolve in water.

Oxygen is used in respiration of plants.

Water (H_2O) is vaporized by the sun.

FUELS

PHYTO-PLANKTON, the floating algae and plants in water

Oxygen is used by bacteria.

Bacteria supply oxygen to plants as nitrates (NO_3).

oxygen during the night. During the day, they give off oxygen by photosynthesis. (*See* PHOTO-SYNTHESIS; RESPIRATION.)

To obtain pure oxygen, air is first cooled until it liquefies. The different gases in the air that have now turned to liquid boil at different temperatures. This allows them to be separated in a process called fractional distillation. (*See* DISTILLATION.) Liquid oxygen is pale blue in color.

When substances react with oxygen, they are said to be oxidized. The body produces energy by oxidizing certain compounds. When fuels burn, they are oxidized. Rust on iron is due to oxidation. (*See* OXIDATION AND REDUCTION; RUST.)

People suffering from severe illness may need more oxygen than normal. They may be placed in special chambers with pure oxygen, or they may breathe in oxygen through tubes connected to an oxygen tank. In welding, acetylene gas is combined with pure oxygen and burned. It gives a very hot flame. Liquid oxygen is used in space rockets to provide power. (*See* OXYACETYLENE TORCH; SPACE TRAVEL.)

Oxygen's atomic number is 8, and its atomic weight is 15.9994. The boiling point of oxygen is -297.2°F. [-182.9°C]. It freezes at -361.1°F. [-218.4°C].   M.E./M.H.M.; J.R.W.

OYSTER (ȯi′stər) Oysters are a type of mollusk found in many seas of the world. Oysters often live on the bottom of oceans, mostly in inlets near shore. (*See* MOLLUSCA.)

The oyster's shell is made up of two parts called valves. Oysters are known as bivalves. (*See* BIVALVE.) A hinge at one end holds the valves together. One valve is deeper and larger than the other, and the oyster's body rests in it. The second valve acts as a lid. The oyster usually keeps its valves slightly opened. If an enemy comes near, the oyster snaps the valves shut.

The mantle, a fleshy organ, lines the inside of the shell, surrounding the body organs. The mantle makes liquid substances that harden and add material to the shell. In this way, the shell becomes larger as the animal grows. Lines on the outside of the shell show the additions of this material from the mantle.

The oyster is a kind of mollusk. Oysters attach themselves to various surfaces, such as aboveground mangrove roots in coastal areas (left).

The oyster's soft body is a grayish mass of tissues containing the body organs. The oyster has no head. The animal uses its gills to breathe and capture food. (*See* GILLS.) Cilia (hairlike parts) of the gills gather tiny organisms from the water and push them toward the oyster's mouth. The mouth is an opening at the narrowest part of the body.

Sometimes, a grain of sand or similar object gets into the shell and rubs against the oyster's body. The mantle covers the object with thin layers of shell material. In this way, a pearl is formed. Pearls used as gems come from special pearl oysters. Pearls produced by the kinds of oysters that are used as food have little value. (*See* PEARL.)

An oyster has many enemies, such as fish, sea stars, crabs, and snails. Human beings are probably the oyster's greatest enemy. More oysters are caught and eaten than any other shellfish. Also, the areas where many oysters live have been damaged by pollution and disease. (*See also* POLLUTION.)

J.J.A./C.S.H.

OZONE (ō′zōn) Ozone (O$_3$) is a dark blue gas. It is an allotrope of oxygen. (*See* ALLOTROPE; OXYGEN.) This means that ozone molecules contain only oxygen atoms, but their number and arrangement are different than in normal oxygen. Normal oxygen has two atoms of oxygen in each molecule. Ozone has three atoms of oxygen in each molecule. The atoms in a molecule of ozone are arranged in a triangle. (*See* ATOM; MOLECULE.) Ozone boils at -168°F. [-111°C] and freezes at -314°F. [-192°C].

Ozone is formed when electricity is passed through the air or through pure oxygen. For example, ozone is formed by sparks in an electric motor or by lightning in a storm. Ozone is also produced in the atmosphere by the action of the sun's rays on normal oxygen. Ozone can be used to sterilize water, to purify air, and to decolorize foods.

Ozone in the stratosphere is very important to the health of animals, especially humans. (*See* ATMOSPHERE.) Ozone absorbs the sun's ultraviolet rays, shielding organisms on

To help understand the effects of ozone pollution, scientists have developed special enclosures that contain high levels of ozone. The enclosure at left is located in the Great Smoky Mountains National Park, which lies on the border between North Carolina and Tennessee. Scientists there are studying the effects of ozone on the park's plants.

earth from their harmful effects. The ozone layer is being destroyed, however, by chemical compounds called chlorofluorocarbons. (*See* CHLOROFLUOROCARBON.) Scientists believe these compounds have already led to a hole in the ozone layer in the atmosphere above the south pole. Without a protective layer of ozone in the stratosphere, ultraviolet rays may cause increases in cases of skin cancer around the world.

When ozone is found in the troposphere, however, it is a pollutant. It is the main gas found in smog. (*See* SMOG.) Ozone is formed in the troposphere when gases from automobile exhaust mix with oxygen in the air and are then struck by the ultraviolet rays in sunshine. Ozone in the troposphere can irritate the eyes and lungs. If the ozone levels are high, even breathing can be dangerous. In large cities, special government agencies, such as California's South Coast Air Quality Management District, continually measure ozone levels. A smog alert or ozone alert may be called if the ozone level becomes dangerous for humans and other animals. During a smog or ozone alert, people are generally advised to stay indoors and avoid exercise.

C.C.; M.E./J.R.W.; L.W.

P

PACK RAT The pack rat, sometimes called a wood rat, is a blunt-faced rodent found in North America. The animal has brownish gray fur and, unlike true rats, a hairy tail. (*See* RAT; RODENT.)

Pack rats usually live in the wild. Western pack rats often live in mountains, building nests on rock ledges. Others live in growths such as cacti. A female has one or two litters a season. Each litter consists of three to six young.

The pack rat gets its name from picking up and hiding small articles, such as nails, silverware, and brightly colored stones. The animal is also known as a trade rat. This is because it often discards an item it is carrying in favor of picking up something else.

J.J.A./J.J.M.

PADDLEFISH (pad′əl fish′) A paddlefish is a primitive freshwater fish that belongs to the family Polyodontidae. It can grow to 6 ft. [1.8 m] in length and more than 99 lb. [45 kg] in weight. The paddlefish gets its name because

The paddlefish is a primitive freshwater fish that has a paddle-shaped projection on the end of its snout. Scientists do not know what purpose the projection serves.

it has a long projection on its snout. The projection is shaped like a canoe paddle. It is not known what the paddle-shaped snout is used for. Some ichthyologists (scientists who study fish) think that the paddlefish may use its paddle to stir up the bottom of a river to find food. The paddlefish is omnivorous, eating such small organisms as algae and plankton. (*See* OMNIVORE.)

Paddlefish were once common in the Missouri River. Their numbers have decreased due to the building of dams and to heavy fishing. People eat smoked paddlefish and make caviar out of paddlefish eggs. Recently, paddlefish from the Missouri River were transferred to rivers in Tennessee, where their numbers are now increasing. Another species of paddlefish is found in China.

S.R.G./E.C.M.

PAIN (pān) Pain is an unpleasant sensation that is usually caused by an injury, disease, or other disorder. It is important because, though disagreeable, it warns the organism that something is wrong.

The sensation of pain is received by special nerve cells called pain receptors. These receptors are located throughout the body as well as in the skin. Pain receptors are connected to nerves that eventually lead to the brain. The brain interprets the signal from the pain receptors, identifying the location and intensity of the pain.

Superficial pain is caused by receptors in the skin. A person can usually tell the exact location of superficial pain because the skin has so many pain receptors. Deep pain—pain from the internal organs—is harder to pinpoint because there are fewer deep pain receptors. Sometimes, deep pain may be referred. Referred pain is felt in a part of the body that is some distance from the actual source of the pain.

Pain can best be overcome by treating the cause. Pain also can be controlled by certain drugs, such as aspirin. Doctors prescribe narcotics for very severe pain. (*See* NARCOTIC.) For chronic (long-term) pain, a surgeon may destroy part of the brain or spinal cord in order to interrupt the pain pathway. Such operations are sometimes successful in relieving the pain. *See also* ANALGESIC; ANESTHETIC; NERVOUS SYSTEM.

A.J.C./J.J.F.; M.H.M.

PAINT (pānt) Paint is a mixture of one or more colored powders and a liquid. The colored powder is called a pigment. (*See* PIGMENT.) The liquid is called a vehicle or binder. The vehicle carries the pigment and allows it to be spread. Many vehicles contain a solvent (substance that can dissolve other substances) or thinner.

There are basically two types of pigments—prime and inert. Prime pigments give paint its color. Inert pigments are materials such as calcium carbonate, clay, mica, or talc. Such substances make paint wear longer when applied.

Vehicles include oils, varnishes, latex, and various types of resins. When a vehicle comes in contact with air, it dries and hardens. This causes paint to become a hard film. This film holds the pigment to the surface that has been painted.

Solvents or thinners are added to paint to make it more liquid. For example, latex paints are thinned with water. These paints are therefore called water-based paints.

Types of paints There are various types of paints that are commonly used. Oil-based paints are often used as outside paints and on woodwork and floors. Such paints often protect wood and metal. Latex paints include wall paints, masonry paints and outside paints. Latex paints are often preferred over oil-based paints, because they are easier to use. Also, with latex paints, the painting equipment (such as brushes) can be easily cleaned using soap and water.

Lacquers are often used to cover automobiles. A lacquer is a paint made up of a solution of resins in a solvent. The solvent dries up after the lacquer is put on. (*See* LACQUER.)

Fire-retardant paints help protect against fire damage. These paints contains chemicals that make the paint puff up when it is near fire. The blister forms a barrier between the flame and the surface.

Metallic paints are made with aluminum or bronze powder. They have many uses, such as on bridges. Wood and plaster primers are used for first coats. These paints fill the tiny openings in the wood or plaster. This allows other paints to stick to the surface without sinking into it. Enamels contain small amounts of pigments. The low pigment content makes the paint dry with a high gloss. Enamels are often used in bathrooms and kitchens, because they are easy to wipe clean.

Manufacture of paints The first step in manufacturing paints is mixing the powdered pigment with the vehicle. A small amount of the vehicle is put into a large mechanical mixer. The powdered pigment is slowly added to the vehicle, making a heavy paste. Then workers put the paste into a mill, or grinder, to break up the pigment particles and scatter them throughout the vehicle. Next workers pour the ground paste into a tank, where it is mechanically mixed with more vehicle and such substances as solvents. The paint is mixed

until it is nearly thin enough for use. A tinter adds a small amount of pigment to give the paint the exact color and shade desired. Finally, the paint is strained through a type of filter to remove any solid bits of dust or dirt. It is poured into a filling tank and finally into the metal cans or plastic tubs in which it is sold.

Application of paints Paints are usually put on in several coats, or layers, one on top of another. The first coat—the primer—prepares the surface for the rest of the paint. The second coat, or undercoat, is heavily charged with pigment and is mat (not glossy or shiny). The finishing coat is sometimes glossy. Some-

Automobile bodies are dipped in a kind of paint called a lacquer to give them a corrosion-resistant, protective coating.

times, only a primer and one additional coat are used. The way in which the paint is put on depends on the type of job. Brushes, rollers, or sprayers may be used, or the article may be dipped or tumbled in paint. Decorative paints dry in the air, but industrial paints are often heat-dried. This process, called stoving, toughens the paint surfaces.

New kinds of paints are always being produced. Chemists and engineers do research to come up with improved types of paints. The amount of paint sold in the United States in one year would cover more than 12,000 sq. mi. [32,000 sq km].

J.J.A./R.W.L.

PALEOBOTANY (pā′lē ō bät′ən ē) Paleobotany is the study of fossil plants. (*See* FOSSIL.) Most plants do not have hard parts that can be preserved in rocks. However, sometimes, impressions of plants are found embedded in clay. Plant remnants are also found petrified. A plant becomes petrified when its decaying cells are replaced by silica or calcium carbonate. The result is an exact duplicate of the original plant.

When plants that lived many years ago died, they were covered with layers of soil or volcanic ash. Later, the plants became petrified—that is, the plant cells were replaced by certain minerals. This produced fossil plants, such as the one above. The study of fossil plants is called paleobotany.

The history of plant life on earth has been traced by paleobotanists. Primitive, plantlike algae existed during Precambrian times. (*See* ALGAE; PRECAMBRIAN TIME.) Psilophytes, the first land plants, existed during the early Devonian period. (*See* DEVONIAN PERIOD; PSILOPHYTE.) During the Pennsylvanian period, huge forests of club mosses, ferns, and horsetails grew. These forests died and decayed, and the remaining organic matter was changed into coal. (*See* COAL; PENNSYLVANIAN PERIOD.) Gymnosperms thrived during the Mesozoic era. In the late Mesozoic era, flowering plants (angiosperms) appeared. (*See* ANGIOSPERM; GYMNOSPERM; MESOZOIC ERA.) Flowering plants are still the dominant land plants on earth. *See also* EVOLUTION; PALEONTOLOGY; PLANT KINGDOM. J.M.C./W.R.S.

PALEOCENE EPOCH (pā′lē ə sēn′ ep′ək) The Paleocene epoch is the earliest subdivision of the Tertiary period in the earth's history. (*See* TERTIARY PERIOD.) It began about 65 million years ago and lasted about 11 million years.

A worldwide warming trend occurred during the Paleocene epoch. By the beginning of this period, the dinosaurs and other giant reptiles of the Mesozoic era had become extinct. Mammals, including primates, became more widespread and diversified. Small reptiles, amphibians, and fish were abundant. Flowering plants flourished during the Paleocene epoch. Deposits of natural gas, oil, and coal formed.

There is evidence suggesting that North America and western Europe were part of one continent during the Paleocene epoch. *See also* CONTINENTAL DRIFT; GEOLOGICAL TIME SCALE.

J.M.C./W.R.S.

PALEOCLIMATOLOGY (pā′ lē ō klī′mə-täl′ə jē) Paleoclimatology is the study of ancient climates, called paleoclimates. Paleoclimatologists try to determine the types of climate that have existed on earth since the earliest geological ages. Since most evidence of paleoclimates is found indirectly through rocks and fossils, the paleoclimatologist has a difficult job. There are, however, several indications of paleoclimates that many scientists consider reliable.

Hot paleoclimates are often indicated by limestone formations, coral reefs, and fossils of tropical plants. Cold paleoclimates are indicated by evidence of glaciation (coverings of ice). This evidence includes masses of rocks and boulders, moraines, fjords, and drumlins. Fossils of conifers are another good indication of a cold paleoclimate. (*See* CORAL; CONIFER; FJORD; GLACIER; LIMESTONE.)

Arid (dry) paleoclimates are indicated by large salt deposits. Other evidence includes well-preserved animal footprints. Humid paleoclimates are indicated by dry lake beds, coal deposits, peat bogs, and fossils of tree ferns. (*See* COAL; FERN; PEAT.)

Many scientists believe that the warm climates of the past occurred because the continents lay closer to the equator than they do today. Eventually, the continents drifted to their present positions. (*See* CONTINENTAL DRIFT.) Some scientists suggest that the sun's radiation has varied because of sunspot activity. (*See* SUNSPOT.)

During the last 600,000 years, there have been at least four ice ages. (*See* ICE AGE.) Paleoclimatologists are working on explanations of why these periods of glaciation occurred. *See also* CLIMATE; FOSSIL; GEOLOGICAL TIME SCALE; PALEOBOTANY.

J.M.C./W.R.S.

PALEONTOLOGY (pā′lē än′täl′ə jē) Paleontology is the study of the fossil remnants of organisms. The study of fossil plants is sometimes considered a separate field called paleobotany. (*See* FOSSIL; PALEOBOTANY.)

Many fossils are found as part of solid rock. This paleontologist, or scientist who studies fossils, is carefully chipping away the surrounding rock to expose a fossil.

Fossils are found in layers of sedimentary rock. (*See* SEDIMENTARY ROCK.) Through complex methods of dating, paleontologists can find out the age of the fossils and thus the age of the rock in which the fossils are found. (*See* DATING.) Paleontologists can also find out whether the rock was formed on land or underwater. Fossils give a good indication of evolutionary processes. (*See* EVOLUTION.) Paleontology is also used in prospecting and geology. *See also* GEOLOGY; PROSPECTING.

J.M.C./W.R.S.

PALEOZOIC ERA (pā′lē ə zō′ik er′ə) The Paleozoic era in the earth's history began about 570 million years ago and lasted about 345 million years. It includes seven geological periods: Cambrian, Ordovician, Silurian, Devonian, Mississippian, Pennsylvanian, and Permian. The Mississippian and Pennsylvanian periods are often combined and called the

The middle Paleozoic era was characterized by the rapid development of fish and the evolution of amphibians. In the warm climate of the Devonian period (about 398 to 345 million years ago) of this era, the first forests began growing in the swamps, rivers and lakes dried up, and many fish died. The lobe-finned fish (above left), however, could breathe air and move about on land using its fins. These fish probably evolved into early amphibians.

Carboniferous period. (*See* CAMBRIAN PERIOD; CARBONIFEROUS PERIOD; DEVONIAN PERIOD; MISSISSIPPIAN PERIOD; ORDOVICIAN PERIOD; PENNSYLVANIAN PERIOD; PERMIAN PERIOD; SILURIAN PERIOD.)

The early Paleozoic era was characterized by algae, trilobites, and other primitive forms of water life. The first fish probably evolved during the Ordovician period. Much of North America was covered by water during the Cambrian and Ordovician periods.

The middle Paleozoic era was characterized by the rapid development of fish and the evolution of amphibians. The first forests grew in the swamps of the Devonian period. Shelled animals and amphibians were abundant by the Mississippian period. Limestone, coal, natural gas, oil, and deposits of iron ore, zinc, and lead formed.

The last two periods of the Paleozoic era are characterized by the development of reptiles and conifers. Some of the primitive organisms of the Cambrian period became extinct. Fish, amphibians, and reptiles were all plentiful by the end of the Permian period. The Ural and Appalachian mountains formed during this time. Large coal deposits also formed during the Pennsylvanian period. *See also* EVOLUTION; GEOLOGICAL TIME SCALE.

J.M.C./W.R.S.

PALLADIUM *See* ELEMENT.

PALM FAMILY The palm (päm) family includes over one thousand species of plants in the tropic and subtropic regions of the world. Although many are low-lying plants with spiral-growing leaves, the best-known

There are more than a thousand different kinds of plants in the palm family. One group, the palm trees (right), provide people with such products as building materials, oils, and food.

species are the palm trees. They can grow 110 ft. [33.3 m] tall. The leaves often grow as long as 40 ft. [12.1 m]. (*See* LEAF.)

Palm trees produce many valuable items used by people. Timber is cut from the trunk. Mats, clothes, and roofs are made from the trunk and leaves. The sap is made into drinks. The fruits of the trees are often delicious. Coconuts and dates are both fruits from palm trees. S.R.G./M.H.S.

PANCREAS (pang′krē əs) The pancreas is an important organ found in the bodies of human beings and all other animals with backbones. The pancreas produces a strong digestive juice that helps break down food in the small intestine. It also produces the hormones insulin and glucagon. (*See* DIGESTION; HORMONE.)

The human pancreas is about 5 to 6 in. [12 to 15 cm] long, 1.5 in. [3.8 cm] wide, and 1 in. [2.5 cm] thick. It lies behind the stomach.

Digestive juices from the pancreas flow into the first part of the small intestine, called the duodenum. (*See* INTESTINE.) The juices contain enzymes that help digest proteins, starches, sugars, and fats. (*See* ENZYME.) The juices are also rich in salts that help neutralize the strong acids secreted by the stomach.

Small clusters of cells, called islets of Langerhans, are scattered throughout the pancreas. They secrete (give off) insulin directly into the bloodstream. The blood carries insulin to cells throughout the body. The cells need insulin to help them use glucose, the sugar that is their main fuel. The islets of Langerhans also secrete glucagon into the blood. Glucagon acts on the liver, causing it to release stored glucose into the blood. *See also* BANTING, SIR FREDERICK; DIABETES; INSULIN.

W.R.P./M.J.C.; J.J.F.; M.H.M.

PANDA (pan′də) A panda is one of two species of omnivorous mammals native to Asia. (*See* MAMMAL; OMNIVORE.) Both of these species have an "extra thumb" on the wrist of the forepaws. This thumb helps the panda strip leaves from branches and hold things in its paws.

The giant panda (*Ailuropoda melanoleuca*) has a white, bearlike body with black hair on its ears, shoulders, and legs and around the

The giant panda (right) is a very rare animal. It lives in the bamboo forests of western China. It may eat more than 20 lb. [9 kg] of food each day.

eyes. It reaches a length of 5 ft. [1.5 m] and a weight of 350 lb. [160 kg]. The giant panda feeds mostly on bamboo and other plants but sometimes eats fish and other small animals. A giant panda may eat more than 20 lb. [9 kg] of food each day. It lives on the ground and stays alone except during mating season. The giant panda is very rare and is protected by law in China. Although some taxonomists classify the giant panda as a member of the raccoon family, other taxononmists classify it as a bear. Still others classify it in a totally separate family.

The lesser panda (*Ailurus fulgens*) is also called the red panda or cat-bear. It is much

The lesser panda (left), or red panda, lives in the mountains of eastern Asia and spends most of the day asleep in trees.

Pangolins live in southeastern Asia, Indonesia, and parts of Africa. When attacked, they roll themselves into a tight ball. They are so heavily armored that few enemies can harm them.

People hunt pangolins for their meat. However, because they are shy and only look for food at night, pangolins are hard to find. *See also* ANTEATER; ARMADILLO.   W.R.P./J.J.M.

The pangolin has few enemies because of its armor.

smaller than the giant panda. Its body is about 24 in. [60 cm] long, and its bushy, ringed tail is about 20 in. [50 cm] long. It weighs about 8.8 lb. [4 kg]. Its fur is reddish brown on the back and black on the belly. Its face has white markings. The lesser panda lives in the mountains of eastern Asia and spends most of the day asleep in the trees. Lesser pandas usually stay in groups of two or more. The lesser panda is classified as a member of the raccoon family. *See also* BEAR; RACCOON.   A.J.C./J.J.M.

PANGOLIN (pang′gə lən) The pangolin, or scaly anteater, is a mammal that belongs to the scaly anteater family, Manidae. (*See* MAMMAL.) Pangolins look like the anteater and the armadillo. They vary in length from 3 to 5 ft. [0.9 to 1.5 m], including their long, strong tail. They have overlapping, horny, brown scales that resemble coats of mail worn by medieval knights. Pangolins are toothless. They have narrow snouts and sticky, ropelike tongues. They can thrust their tongues far out to catch the termites and ants on which they feed.

PANTOGRAPH (pant′ə graf′) A pantograph is an instrument used by artists and draftspersons for copying a design or plan onto a sheet of paper. A pantograph is made up of a number of rods. These rods are joined together by pins that can be adjusted. A pointer is moved over the lines of the design or plan. This movement is transferred by the rods to a pencil or pen at the other end. This traces out a copy of the original drawing. The size of the copy can be altered by adjusting the position of the rods.   M.E./R.W.L.

PROJECT

PAPER Paper is one of the most useful materials ever invented. The product is involved in nearly every aspect of people's everyday lives. Books, magazines, and newspapers are printed on paper. Education, government, and industry could not operate without paper.

The world's first maker of paper was the wasp. The wasp chews tiny pieces of wood until they form a pulp. The wasp then spits out the wet pulp and smooths it into a thin sheet. When the pulp dries, it becomes paper. It is used by certain kinds of wasps to build their homes. (*See* WASP.)

Paper gets its name from papyrus, a sheet made by pressing together the core material (pith) of the Egyptian papyrus plant. Papyrus as a writing material was first developed about 6,000 years ago in Egypt. It was not until about 2,000 years later that paper, as it is known today, was invented. The Chinese were the inventors of this paper.

Paper is made of cellulose fibers. Cellulose is a substance found in most plants. (*See* CELLULOSE.) Various types of trees, cotton plants, rice and wheat straws, cornstalks, hemp, and jute are used for making paper.

Most of the paper produced in the United States comes from wood pulp. This pulp is obtained from trees and waste materials of lumbering operations. Some paper is made from pulp recycled from waste paper.

How paper is made For many years, rags were the main raw material for paper. Today, rags have been largely replaced by wood pulp. Wood pulp comes from softwood trees such as pine, spruce, and hemlock. Most wood pulp is made by one of two processes: mechanical or chemical.

The mechanical process is used mainly for the production of inexpensive papers, such as paper on which newspapers are printed. In this process, debarked logs are pressed against a revolving grindstone. The grindstone chips the log into fine pieces that make up wood pulp.

The chief chemical processes for making pulp from wood are the sulfite, sulfate, and soda processes. In all of these processes, the wood is thoroughly washed with water and cut into chips. In the sulfite process, the wood chips are cooked in a digester, which is a closed tank. The chips cook in a solution of calcium bisulfide under steam pressure until the wood forms a pulp. In the sulfate process, the wood is cooked in a solution of caustic soda and sodium sulfide. In the soda process, the wood chips are cooked with caustic soda solution to dissolve the materials that hold the cellulose fibers together.

The pulp produced by the above processes is screened, washed, and bleached. Then it is dried and pressed into sheets. Most paper is made on the Fourdrinier machine. This machine consists of a belt of wire mesh on which watery pulp is spread. The belt passes through a series of rollers, which press the water out of

Paper pulp that is first bleached, as shown above, is used to make white or other light-colored papers.

the pulp. The belt then passes under a turning cylinder called a dandy roll. The dandy roll gives the paper a woven or flat surface. Near the end of the machine, the belt passes through two felt-covered couching rolls, which press out more water. It then goes through two sets of smooth metal press rolls. The press rolls give the paper a smooth finish. The last step before cutting is calendaring, or pressing the paper between chilled rollers. Calendaring gives the paper an even smoother finish, called a machine finish. At the end of the Fourdrinier machine, the paper is wound on spools into large rolls. The paper can then be slit into strips and cut into sheets.

As paper is made, it is usually wound into large rolls (above). The paper is later slit into strips and cut into sheets.

"Water marking," for good quality writing paper, is done by pressing a design into the moist paper at the "wet end" of the machine. Tissue paper is made in the same way as ordinary paper except that it is scraped by a knife edge as it leaves the drying rollers, giving a tissuey finish.

Chemical engineers have found many ways of treating paper to make it strong, fireproof, and resistant to liquids and acids. As a result, paper can, in many instances, replace cloth, metal, and wood. For example, specially treated paper is used to make clothing, such as surgical gowns and disposable diapers. The average person in the United States uses about 680 lb. [308 kg] of paper and paperboard every year.

Paper recycling Paper recycling is the use of waste paper to make new paper. Such discarded items as grocery bags and newspapers are collected, cleaned, and made into pulp. The pulp can be used in making such products as newsprint, paperboard, tissue paper, and writing paper. Beginning in the 1960s, a growing concern about pollution promoted greater recycling efforts to reduce solid wastes. In the following years, the recycling of paper continued to gain importance as concerns about vanishing forests grew. (*See* DEFORESTATION; ENVIRONMENT; FORESTRY.) Many communities now have waste recycling programs that encourage or require households and businesses to recycle most of the paper products they use. Cardboard, newspaper, computer paper, and white and colored office paper can all be recycled. *See also* RECYCLING.

J.J.A.; C.C./F.W.S.; L.W.

PARACHUTE (par′ə shüt′) A parachute looks similar to a large umbrella but is made of a light fabric. It is used to slow down the fall of a person or object from an airplane in flight or from any great height.

A parachute operates on simple principles. There are two forces that act upon any falling object—air resistance and gravity. Gravity pulls the object quickly toward the earth. Air, however, resists the object's downward movement. At low speeds, the pull of gravity is much stronger than the resistance of air. Thus, air resistance has little effect. However, air resistance becomes larger as the speed of fall increases. Eventually, when air resistance and the pull of gravity balance, the object reaches a speed called terminal velocity. From that point on, the object falls with constant speed. Large, flat surfaces offer a greater area of resistance than do thin, sharp surfaces. Therefore, an object shaped like a saucer reaches its terminal velocity sooner, so it falls much more slowly than one shaped like a needle. (*See* GRAVITY.)

Parachutes designed for human use are made of nylon. In the early years of aviation, parachutes where made of silk. The average parachute is about 24 to 28 ft. [7 to 9 m] across when open. Parachutes for cargo may be as large as 100 ft. [30 m] across.

Parachutes for human use are worn on a harness that consists of a series of straps fitted around the shoulders and legs of the parachutist. The parachute is tightly packed into a compact bundle with a canvas cover. It is worn either as a seat pack (to be sat on) or as a chest or back pack.

Special straps, called risers, are attached to the shoulder portion of the harness. They hold the shrouds, or lines, that are attached to the canopy, which is the umbrellalike part of the parachute. A ring for pulling the rip cord is attached to one of the straps. The rip cord opens the parachute pack. When the cord is pulled, the parachute springs out of its tight confinement, and the air forces it open. Some-

Sometimes, parachutes are used as extra "brakes" to slow down aircraft that are landing at high speeds.

times, a special line, called a static line, is used to open a parachute. The static line is attached to the airplane. When the parachutist jumps from the airplane, the static line pulls open the parachute automatically, and then releases itself. The static line is usually used in military aircraft that carry large numbers of paratroopers (soldiers).

As soon as the parachute canopy opens completely, the air slows the descent of the parachutist so quickly that he or she may be jerked sharply. Parachutes with slots in their canopies have been developed to reduce the force of this opening shock.

Parachutists descend at the rate of about 15 ft. [5 m] per second, or slightly faster. Parachute drops from less than 500 ft. [150 m] above the ground are dangerous because this height does not allow the parachute time to open. Parachutists can control the direction of their descent by pulling on the shrouds. Parachutists often land with great force. Heavy boots and special shock-absorbing techniques help prevent sprained ankles and broken legs. Experienced parachutists can often land very lightly in a standing position.

Parachute jumping has become a popular sport in the United States and Europe. There are many clubs and national and international jumping events in which parachutists try to land on small targets on the ground.

W.R.P./R.W.L.

PARAFFIN (par′ə fən) Paraffin is a white, waxy, solid hydrocarbon mixture that has no taste or odor. (*See* HYDROCARBON.)

Paraffin is made from a mixture of petroleum fractions, which are products separated from petroleum. (*See* PETROLEUM.) The fractions are chilled and pressed through a filter to remove heavy oil. The remaining solid is

paraffin wax. Paraffin wax is used to put a waterproof coating on cardboard containers such as milk cartons. Paraffin wax is also the main ingredient in candles.

Ordinary paraffin wax melts at 90° to 150°F. [32° to 66°C]. Microcrystalline paraffin wax is another type of paraffin wax. It melts at 150 to 185°F. [66 to 85°C].

Paraffin wax is used in certain kinds of polishes and as a moisture-proof coating on textiles. Jars in which food is preserved are often sealed with paraffin wax.

W.R.P./J.M.

PARAKEET (par′ə kēt′) A parakeet is a bird that belongs to the parrot family, Psittacidae. A parakeet is a small parrot with a long tail. (*See* PARROT.) There are several species in the world. Most wild parakeets live in Australia, India, Africa, and other tropical regions. Parakeets eat flowers, fruits, and seeds. They are very colorful and are often kept as pets. The Carolina parakeet, once found in the United States, is now extinct. *See also* EXTINCTION.

S.R.G./L.L.S.

PARALLAX (par′ə laks′) Suppose that you are looking at an object against a background. As you move your head, the object seems to move against the background. This effect is called parallax. In astronomy, parallax is used to find the distances of the planets and the nearer stars from earth.

To measure distance from the earth to a planet using parallax, the position of the planet is first measured at a particular time relative to the background of the stars. Then the planet's position is measured again twelve hours later. In this time, the measuring instrument has moved in space because of the earth's rotation and revolution. Because of the earth's movement, the planet seems to move against the background of stars. The amount that it moves depends on the planet's distance from earth. Therefore, its distance can be calculated.

To measure distance between the earth and a nearby star using parallax, the positions of the star are measured six months apart. In this time, the earth has moved around to the opposite side of the sun. This large movement of the earth produces a small apparent movement in the star. Therefore, the star's distance from earth can be measured.

Parallax can cause inaccuracies when a person reads the dial on a scientific instrument. The pointer on the dial is always a small distance away from the scale. If the person reads the dial at an angle, the pointer gives a wrong reading because of parallax. This can be overcome by having a mirror on the scale. The pointer is lined up with its reflection. This assures that the person is directly above the pointer when taking a reading and, thus, the reading will be accurate. M.E./S.S.B.

PARALYSIS (pə ral′ə səs) Paralysis is the loss of use of muscles. Sometimes, a whole group of muscles becomes completely paralyzed. Other times, muscles can respond at a reduced level, causing only partial paralysis.

Paralysis itself is not a disease. It is caused by disease in the muscles or damage to the brain or to the nerves that stimulate the muscles. For instance, if a person has a badly damaged spinal cord, there will be paralysis of all the muscles below the injury. If the nerves that carry messages back to the brain are also affected, there will be no feeling in the lower half of the body. (*See* NERVOUS SYSTEM.)

Doctors divide paralysis into two main types: spastic paralysis and flaccid paralysis.

In spastic paralysis, the muscles affected are tense, as though they were pulling. However, the muscles are weak and cannot be controlled. Spastic paralysis is usually due to damage in the brain or the upper part of the spinal cord. In flaccid paralysis, the muscles are limp and flabby. Flaccid paralysis is due to damage to nerves lower down in the nervous system. Poliomyelitis causes this type of paralysis. (*See* POLIOMYELITIS.)

When paralysis continues for a long time, the nerves and the muscles become permanently useless. The nerve cells die, and the muscles become thin and wasted. To prevent this, electrical treatment can be given by physical therapists to keep the muscles active. The electrical impulse makes the muscles contract. However, the patient does not regain control of the muscle contractions. *See also* MUSCLE. D.M.H.W./J.J.F.; M.H.M.

PARAMECIUM (par′ə mē′shē əm) The paramecium is a one-celled organism that lives in fresh water. It is a protozoan and belongs to the kingdom Protista. (*See* PROTISTA; PROTOZOA.)

Because of its slipperlike shape, the paramecium is sometimes called a slipper animalcule. Its body is covered with tiny, hairlike cilia, which it uses for movement and for feeding. (*See* CILIUM.) On one side of the organism is an oral groove, which leads to the mouth and gullet. Cilia on this groove create a flow of blue-green algae, bacteria, and other tiny organisms into the mouth. Food is digested in food vacuoles at the end of the gullet. (*See* VACUOLE.) Wastes from digestion are ejected through an anal pore (opening). There are two or three contractile vacuoles located near the surface at the ends of the paramecium. These contractile vacuoles regulate the amount of water inside the paramecium and get rid of metabolic wastes by squirting the water and wastes out of the cell. (*See* METABOLISM.)

The body of the paramecium has a rigid outer membrane called a pellicle. Just inside the pellicle is a layer of firm, clear cytoplasm called ectoplasm. The watery part of the cytoplasm with its various structures is called endoplasm. (*See* CYTOPLASM; ECTOPLASM; ENDOPLASM.)

The paramecium (above) is a one-celled organism found in fresh water.

The paramecium has one large nucleus called the macronucleus and one or more smaller nuclei called the micronuclei (nuclei is plural for *nucleus*). The macronucleus controls most of the cell's activities and contains genes. The micronucleus also contains genes and functions in sexual reproduction. Paramecia (plural of *paramecium*) usually repro-

duce asexually by dividing into two new organisms. (*See* ASEXUAL REPRODUCTION; GENE; REPRODUCTION.) Occasionally, paramecia reproduce sexually in a process called conjugation. Two paramecia line up next to each other, exchange micronuclei, separate, and divide several times. Conjugation has a revitalizing effect on paramecia. Without conjugation, a paramecium grows old and dies. *See also* CELL.   A.J.C./M.J.C.; C.S.H.

PARASITE (par′ə sīt′) A parasite is an organism that lives with or inside another organism —called the host—in order to feed or find shelter. Some parasites eat the flesh of the host. Others eat the food that the host has eaten. Other parasites just live in or on the host for safety. Parasites always harm the host, though they rarely kill it. If they did kill the host, the parasites would destroy their home and source for food. However, parasites often weaken the host to the point where it may die of other causes, such as disease. Some parasites have parasites—smaller organisms called hyperparasites—within them.

The tiny red mite pictured on the harvestman, or daddy longlegs, at left is a parasite. It is feeding on the harvestman, which is its host.

Animal parasites Nearly every animal on earth has parasites. The average human being has several parasites in his or her body. Also, nearly every major phylum of animals includes species that are parasitic. Most of the animal parasites belong to the phyla (plural of *phylum*) Platyhelminthes, Aschelminthes, and Arthropoda. In addition, many protozoans, which are one-celled, animallike organisms in the kingdom Protista, are parasites. (*See* ARTHROPODA; ASCHELMINTHES; PLATYHELMINTHES; PROTOZOA.)

Ectoparasites live on the outside of their hosts. One well-known ectoparasite is the flea. (*See* FLEA.) The flea is an insect that lives in the fur and feathers of animals. It feeds by sticking its sharp "beak" into the animals' skin and sucking out blood. Besides causing an irritation to the host, fleas can also spread serious diseases. The plague is a disease caused by bacteria spread by fleas that live on rats. In the 1300s, an epidemic of plague called the Black Death killed millions of Europeans. (*See* EPIDEMIC.)

Other well-known ectoparasites include ticks, leeches, and mosquitoes. (*See* LEECH; MOSQUITO; TICK.) Leeches, ticks, and mosquitoes, unlike fleas, do not spend all their time on the host. They land on the skin, puncture the skin with their beak, suck out some of the host's blood, and leave. Mosquitoes often spread disease and endoparasites between hosts.

Endoparasites are parasites that live and feed inside the bodies of their hosts. They feed on blood, tissue, tissue fluids, and the food of the hosts. Endoparasites are responsible for some of the world's most serious diseases, such as malaria and sleeping sickness. (*See* MALARIA.) Malaria and sleeping sickness are caused by microscopic, one-celled organisms that live in the bloodstream of mammals. They are spread by biting insects.

Many endoparasites are worms. Tapeworms live in the intestines of their host. (*See* TAPEWORM.) They attach themselves to the host by means of suckers or hooks. The worms absorb through their skin some of the digested food from the host. Eggs of the tapeworms pass through the host's body in the feces. The next generation of tapeworms hatches from the eggs and spreads to other animals.

Another parasitic worm—the blood fluke—lives in the blood of its host. When the worms lay their eggs inside the host, serious injury and even death may occur. The condition caused by the blood fluke is called schistosomiasis. (*See* SCHISTOSOMIASIS.)

Social parasites Parasites that affect a group of organisms—rather than just one organism—are called social parasites. The best-known social parasites are the cuckoos of Europe, Asia, and Africa. (*See* CUCKOO.) These birds lay their eggs in the nests of other birds. The young cuckoos hatch along with the host's own young. However, the young cuckoo is usually more aggressive than the other young birds. It may demand more food or even push the other young birds out of the nest. The cuckoo becomes stronger than the host's own young. In this way, the entire population of host birds is affected. Some bees and wasps are social parasites, too.

Parasitic plants The reason that there are fewer plant parasites is that most plants are able to produce their own food by photosynthesis. (*See* PHOTOSYNTHESIS.) Therefore, most plants do not need to parasitize other organisms. However, some plants cannot make their own food and have evolved as parasites.

The dodder is one such plant parasite. It is a simple plant that resembles pink cotton. It winds itself around other plants, sends suckers into the other plants, and absorbs food. Mistletoe is another parasitic plant. It can produce food by photosynthesis, but it must get its water and minerals from trees that it grows on. (*See* MISTLETOE.)

Parasites can sometimes be useful for controlling insect or plant pests. The study of parasites is called parasitology.

S.R.G./M.J.C.; T.L.G.; M.H.M; C.R.N.

PARENCHYMA (pə reng′kə mə) Parenchyma is living plant tissue that is made up of thin-walled, fourteen-sided cells. The cells are not specialized, but some will undergo differentiation. (*See* DIFFERENTIATION, CELLULAR.) Parenchyma cells may be either loosely or densely packed.

Leaf parenchyma cells contain chlorophyll and make up the tissues in which most photosynthesis takes place. (*See* CHLOROPHYLL; LEAF; PHOTOSYNTHESIS.) The cortex (outer part) and pith (inner part) of stems and roots is composed of parenchyma cells. (*See* CORTEX.) The soft, fleshy tissues of fruits are also made of parenchyma. (*See* FRUIT.) Collenchyma and sclerenchyma develop from parenchyma. *See also* COLLENCHYMA: SCLERENCHYMA.

A.J.C./M.J.C.; M.H.S.

PARROT (par′ət) A parrot is a bird that belongs to the family Psittacidae. It is a stout bird with a heavy bill and strong talons (claws). Most parrots are very colorful. They live in the forests of tropical and subtropical regions throughout the world. There are over three hundred species. They eat seeds, nuts, buds, fruit, and nectar. Related smaller species of parrots are called parakeets.

Most parrots, such as the pair above, are brightly colored. They live in tropical and subtropical areas throughout the world, and many are kept as pets.

Parrots are commonly kept as pets. They may be taught how to talk, because they can easily imitate various sounds.

S.R.G./L.L.S.

PARSEC (pär′sek′) A parsec is the distance to a star whose position seems to shift by 1 second of arc when viewed from opposite sides of the earth's orbit. (*See* PARALLAX.) A parsec is equal to 3.26 light-years or 19.2 trillion mi. [30.9 trillion km]. (*See* LIGHT-YEAR.) The term *parsec* comes from the words *parallax* and *second.*

Parsecs are used to measure distances in the universe. Proxima Centauri, the nearest star to the sun, is about 1.3 parsecs away. The sun is about 8,000 parsecs from the center of the galaxy. J.M.C./C.R.

PARSLEY FAMILY The parsley (pär′slē) family includes about 1,500 species of herbaceous plants, most of which live in northern temperate regions. They have dark green, compound leaves growing in clusters around a hollow stem. (*See* HERBACEOUS PLANT; LEAF.) The flowers are usually greenish white and grow in clusters at the tip of the stem. (*See* INFLORESCENCE.)

The parsley plant (*Petroselinum crispum*) is a biennial plant native to the Mediterranean area. (*See* BIENNAL PLANT.) It has been introduced worldwide. The leaves of this plant are used fresh or dried as a garnish or flavoring for food. It is a good source of iron and vitamins A and C. Other members of the parsley family include the carrot, celery, and parsnip. This family is sometimes called the carrot family. *See also* HERB.

A.J.C./M.H.S.

PARSNIP (pär′snəp) Parsnip (*Pastinaca sativa*) is a biennial herbaceous plant belonging to the parsley family. (*See* BIENNIAL PLANT; HERBACEOUS PLANT; PARSLEY FAMILY.) It has lobed leaves and yellow flowers. (*See* LEAF.) Parsnip is cultivated for its large, white, carrot-shaped tap root. (*See* ROOT.) The root is harvested after the first growing season and is usually served as a cooked vegetable. It is rich in carbohydrates and vitamins A and C.

A.J.C./F.W.S.

PARTHENOGENESIS (pär′thə nō jen′ə səs) Parthenogenesis is a type of asexual reproduction in which an unfertilized egg develops into a mature organism. It is common among lower plants and some invertebrate animals, such as rotifers and insects. (*See* INSECT; ROTIFER.) Some types of ants, bees, and wasps, for example, develop by parthenogenesis. Most invertebrates capable of parthenogenesis are also capable of sexual reproduction. Parthenogenesis can be artificially caused in many animals—vertebrates and invertebrates —by treating the unfertilized egg with special chemicals. *See also* ASEXUAL REPRODUCTION; REPRODUCTION. A.J.C./C.R.N.

PARTICLE ACCELERATORS *See* ACCELERATORS, PARTICLE.

PARTICLE PHYSICS (pärt′i kəl fiz′iks) All matter is made up of tiny particles called atoms. (*See* ATOM.) For many years, scientists thought that atoms were the smallest particles of matter. They thought that atoms had no structure. It is now known that atoms are themselves made up of even smaller particles. The main particles that make up atoms are called protons, neutrons, and electrons. (*See* ELECTRON; NEUTRON; PROTON.) They are known as subatomic particles. Since these three particles were discovered, many more subatomic particles have been found. The study of these particles is called particle physics.

Early discoveries The first subatomic particle to be discovered was the electron. Physicists soon realized that the electron was smaller than an atom. Then they discovered that atoms contain electrons. This meant that the atom had to have some sort of structure. Atoms were no longer thought to be the smallest particles that could exist. In 1911, the British physicist Ernest Rutherford did an experiment to investigate the structure of the atom. (*See* RUTHERFORD, ERNEST.) Through this experiment, Rutherford found that atoms contain a very small core called a nucleus. (*See* NUCLEUS, ATOMIC.) He found that almost all of the mass of an atom was contained in its nucleus. The nucleus is surrounded by a number of electrons. The nucleus and the electrons together make up the atom.

Rutherford's theory also explained that the nucleus of a hydrogen atom contained just one particle. This particle is called the proton. It was the second subatomic particle to be discovered. The proton has 1,860 times the mass that an electron has. (*See* MASS.) The electron and the proton have equal and opposite electric charges. The electron has a negative charge, and the proton has a positive charge. Atoms have equal numbers of protons and electrons. Thus, electric charge is balanced out in the atom.

However, at first, scientists could not understand how the charges balanced. The nuclei of all the atoms seem to contain too many protons to balance out the charge of the electrons. For example, the nucleus of an oxygen atom is just about sixteen times as heavy as a proton. Therefore, scientists concluded the oxygen nucleus has sixteen protons. However, they knew that the oxygen atom has only eight electrons. If it also had sixteen protons, it would have an electric charge. However, oxygen atoms do not have an electric charge. Therefore, scientists concluded that there must be particles in the nucleus besides protons. They named these other particles *neutrons.* They deduced that the neutron is slightly heavier than the proton and has no electric charge. An oxygen nucleus contains eight protons and eight neutrons. This gives a total mass equal to about sixteen protons. Because there are eight protons to balance eight electrons, the oxygen atom has no electric charge. In 1932, British physicist Sir James Chadwick confirmed the existence of the neutron by experiment. (*See* CHADWICK, SIR JAMES.)

The strong nuclear force Realizing that the nucleus contained both protons and neutrons solved the riddle about the atom's mass and neutral charge. However, physicists still had

The development of particle detectors has allowed physicists to analyze in great detail the behavior of subatomic particles. Shown is a display of particle trails produced by a detector.

other questions about the atomic nucleus. For example, two bodies with a positive charge repel each other, or push each other away. Therefore, scientists assumed that the protons in the nucleus should repel each other because they all have a positive charge. In this case, the nucleus would fly apart. However, the nucleus is really very stable. Physicists realized that there must be a very strong force holding the nucleus together. This force must be strong enough to overcome the repulsion between the protons. Physicists named this force the strong nuclear force. It only works over very short distances, about equal to the width of the nucleus. This is about 10^{-13} cm. (10^{-13} is one divided by ten thirteen times.) The strong nuclear force is caused by tiny particles called gluons. The other recognized fundamental forces affecting matter are gravity, electromagnetism, and the weak nuclear force. (*See* FORCE.)

Properties of particles Since 1947, hundreds of particles have been discovered. One way of discovering new particles is by examining cosmic rays. (*See* COSMIC RAYS.) Another important method is to use a large machine called a particle accelerator. (*See* ACCELERATORS, PARTICLE.) In a particle accelerator, streams of particles are made to travel at very high speeds. The particles then hit other particles or a target consisting of a small amount of an element. New subatomic particles or elements may then be formed. (*See* ELEMENT.)

Subatomic particles can be measured in different ways. They all have a rest mass. This is the mass of the particle when it is still. When it is moving very fast, its mass increases. (*See* RELATIVITY.) Many particles have an electric charge. This charge can be either positive or negative. Many particles also have spin. They spin much the same way a football does when it is thrown. The spin, mass, and charge are all fixed for each particle.

Subatomic particles are made up of elementary particles. An elementary particle cannot be broken down into smaller particles, and its size is too small to measure. All elementary particles have an antiparticle. These antiparticles have the same mass, but they have the opposite charge or spin as the original particle. For example, the antiparticle of the electron is called the positron. It has the same mass as an electron but has a positive charge. A particle and an antiparticle can exist for a very short time together. However, they soon collide and destroy each other. As they destroy each other, they give off a gamma ray. (*See* ANTIMATTER; GAMMA RAY.)

Subatomic particles fall into one of two classes. One class, called fermions, is made up of those particles that make up matter. (*See* MATTER.) Fermions can be divided into hadrons and leptons, depending on which of the four fundamental forces act on them. Hadrons are made up of quarks and are acted upon by the strong nuclear force. (*See* QUARK.) Hadron particles called baryons, which include protons and neutrons, are made up of three quarks each. Hadron particles called mesons are made up of a quark and an antiquark. (*See* MESON.) Leptons can be divided into electrically charged particles and uncharged particles. Leptons are acted upon by the electromagnetic force and the weak nuclear force. Electrically charged leptons include the electron, the muon, and the tau particle. The uncharged leptons include the neutrinos. (*See* NEUTRINO.) Neutrinos can be transformed into charged leptons by colliding them with atomic nuclei (plural of *nucleus*). The electron neutrino can be transformed into an electron. The muon neutrino can be transformed into a muon. The tau neutrino can be transformed into a tau.

The other class of particles, called bosons, is made up of those particles that transmit forces. There are four known kinds of bosons —photons, gluons, gravitons, and weakons. Photons transmit the electromagnetic force. (*See* PHOTON.) Gluons transmit the strong nuclear force. Gravitrons transmit gravity. (*See* GRAVITY.) Weakons transmit the weak nuclear force. In the 1980s, scientists proved that the electromagnetic force and the weak nuclear force are two forms of the same force.

The standard model theory Studies of a certain kind of weakon particle that was created in 1989 in particle accelerators confirm much of what scientists call the standard model theory of particle physics. According to this theory, all matter in the universe seems to occur in one of three generations, or categories. Each generation seems to be made up of combinations of two types of quarks, a charged lepton, and an uncharged lepton.

The first generation of matter is made up of the quarks called *up* and *down,* an electron, and an electron neutrino. The second generation of matter is made up of the *strange* and *charm* quarks, the muon, and the muon neutrino. The third generation of matter is made up of the *top* and *bottom* quarks, the tau, and the tau neutrino. The second and third generations of matter occur only as a result of events involving large amounts of energy, such as those events that occur in particle accelerators. This makes it difficult to observe the particles that make up these two generations. The top quark, for example, has never been observed. Scientists have only predicted its existence. Research in particle physics now centers on

proving the existence of missing particles and determining why particles have the masses they have.

C.C.; M.E./J.T.; L.W.

PASCAL, BLAISE (1623-1662) Blaise Pascal was a French scientist, mathematician, philosopher, and theologian. He did original work in many different fields. He studied atmospheric pressure and made an important discovery in hydrostatics. (*See* HYDROSTATICS.)

Blaise Pascal

His discovery is now known as Pascal's law. It states that pressures applied to a contained liquid are transmitted equally throughout the liquid, in every direction. He also studied the mathematical theory of probability. (*See* PROBABILITY.) One of his discoveries in probability is called Pascal's triangle. *See also* PASCAL'S TRIANGLE.

M.E./D.G.F.

PASCAL'S TRIANGLE (pas kalz′ trī′ang gəl) Pascal's triangle is an arrangement of numbers shaped like a triangle. It was discovered by the French scientist and mathematician Blaise

Pascal in the 1600s. (*See* PASCAL, BLAISE.) The triangle consists of rows of numbers. The top row has two numbers, 1 and 1. Then each row starts and ends in 1. Two numbers next to each other in a row are added together. The number formed is placed in the row beneath the two numbers and halfway between them.

For example, the third row of Pascal's triangle is 1 3 3 1. The first number in the row beneath is 1. The second number is given by 1 + 3. This number is 4. The third number is given by 3 + 3 and is 6. In the same way, the fourth number is 4, and the last is 1. Therefore, this row is 1 4 6 4 1. The number of rows in Pascal's triangle can be infinite (endless).

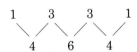

Pascal's triangle can be used in a number of different situations. For example, it can be used to determine probabilities when throwing a number of coins. Pascal's triangle will predict the probability of different combinations of heads and tails turning up. (*See* PROBABILITY.) Suppose that you have three coins. If they are thrown, there are four possible outcomes. You can have three heads, two heads and one tail, one head and two tails, or three tails. As there are four possibilities, you need to look at the row in Pascal's triangle that has four numbers. This is the row 1 3 3 1. These numbers tell you the probability of each combination occurring. 1, 3, 3, and 1 add up to 8. Therefore, there is 1 chance in 8 of throwing three heads, 3 chances in 8 of throwing two heads, 3 chances in 8 for one head, and 1 chance in 8 for no heads. The chances are the same for throwing three, two, one, or no tails with three coins.   M.E./S.P.A.

PASSIONFLOWER (pash′ən flau′er) The passionflower is any of about five hundred species of dicotyledonous flowering plants belonging to genus *Passiflora* in the passionflower family, Passifloraceae. Most are tendril-bearing climbing plants that live in the tropics. (*See* CLIMBING PLANT; DICOTYLEDON.)

The flowers of these plants have an unusual and beautiful appearance. They vary in size from 0.4 to 6 in. [1 to 15 cm] in diameter. There are five petals and five sepals, all of which are similar in color. Inside the petals

The approximately five hundred species of passionflowers produce unusual looking flowers such as the one above. The flower's five stamens and three styles are clearly evident in this picture.

are one or more rings of brightly colored, threadlike filaments. In the center of the flower is a reproductive stalk called a gynophore. About halfway up the gynophore is a ring of five stamens. Above this ring is the ovary with three styles. Each style ends in a large, lobed stigma, giving it the appearance of a large nail or spike. (*See* FLOWER.)

The passionflower produces an edible fruit—the passionfruit. This fruit is sometimes squeezed for its juice or mixed in fruit punch.   A.J.C./M.H.S.

PASTEUR, LOUIS (1822-1895) Louis Pasteur was a French biologist and chemist. Pasteur discovered that yeast causes grape juice to ferment into wine. He also discovered that a similar process causes milk to go sour, butter to turn rancid, and wine to turn into vinegar. (*See* FERMENTATION.) He developed a process called pasteurization. In pasteurization, food is preserved by heating it to kill disease-causing microorganisms. (*See* MICROORGAN-

Louis Pasteur

ISM; PASTEURIZATION.) He also developed a vaccine for rabies. (*See* RABIES; VACCINATION.) He used his vaccine to save the life of a child who had been bitten by a rabid dog. In 1888, he founded the Pasteur Institute, which is a center for medical research. The institute is still in existence today.   M.E./D.G.F.

PASTEURIZATION (pas′chə rə zā′shən) Pasteurization is a method of preserving food by heating it to kill disease-causing microorganisms in it. (*See* MICROORGANISM; PATHOGEN.) The food is then stored in cool conditions. Pasteurization is named after its inventor, Louis Pasteur, a French chemist. (*See* PASTEUR, LOUIS.) Pasteurization is most commonly used for milk but may also be used for cheese, beer, and other foods.

For milk, the process of pasteurization traditionally has involved heating the milk to at least 145°F. [63°C] for not less than thirty minutes. Then the milk is quickly chilled to 50°F. [10°C] or less. This kills most of the bacteria in the milk and allows it to stay fresh for several days. The process does not affect the taste of the milk. Modern dairies use a faster method in which the milk is heated to at least 161°F. [72°C] for fifteen seconds, then cooled. *See also* FOOD PROCESSING; MILK.

W.R.P./C.R.N.

PATELLA (pə tel′ə) The patella, or kneecap, is a small, flat, triangular bone located on the front of the knee. It protects the knee joint. The patella is not directly connected to any other bone. It is held in place by muscle attachments and ligaments. *See also* BONE; LIGAMENT; MUSCLE.   W.R.P./J.J.F.; M.H.M.

PATHOGEN (path′ə jən) Pathogens are organisms that cause disease. Many kinds of bacteria, viruses, fungi, and protozoans are pathogens. *See also* DISEASE.   P.Q.F./J.E.P.

PATHOLOGY (pə thäl′ə jē) Pathology is the study of disease or of any condition that limits health. Pathologists used advanced scientific methods, such as electron microscopy, to help them recognize the changes caused by disease in the tissues and organs of the body. (*See* ELECTRON MICROSCOPE.)

Tests by pathologists help physicians diagnose a disease and the extent of its attack. These tests may include the examination of the blood, urine, and tissues. The use of laboratory tests to diagnose disease is called clinical pathology. Pathologists also study diseased parts removed by surgery. For example, persons suspected of having cancer sometimes have the diseased part removed by surgery. It is then analyzed by a pathologist. If the removed part is malignant, or cancerous, further surgery or special treatment may be necessary. Pathologists also examine corpses to determine the exact cause of death. This examination is called an autopsy.

Comparative pathology is a branch of pathology that compares human diseases with animal diseases. Plant pathology is the study of the diseases of plants. *See also* DISEASE; FORENSIC SCIENCE. W.R.P./J.J.F.

PAULI, WOLFGANG (1900-1958) Wolfgang Pauli was an Austrian physicist. He was born in Vienna and studied in Munich, Germany. Later, he worked in the United States. He made important discoveries about the atom. He also worked on a branch of physics called quantum theory. (*See* ATOM; QUANTUM THEORY.) In 1930, Pauli deduced that there exists a particle called the neutrino. (*See* NEUTRINO.) Pauli studied the radioactive process called beta decay and realized that some unknown particle was being given off. He calculated that the particle should have spin but no mass. He called this particle the neutrino. The neutrino's existence was confirmed by experiment twenty-six years later. Pauli won the Nobel Prize for physics in 1945 for his work in quantum theory. *See also* PARTICLE PHYSICS; RADIOACTIVITY. M.E./D.G.F.

PAULING, LINUS (1901-) is an American chemist known for his studies of chemical bonding. When two atoms combine to form a molecule, they are held together by a bond. Atoms combine by means of small particles called electrons. All atoms have electrons. (*See* ATOM; ELECTRON; MOLECULE.)

There are different kinds of bonds. In one kind, called the covalent bond, two atoms share some of their electrons. Pauling discovered that these electrons are shared in pairs. A pair of electrons spends part of the time with one atom and part of the time with the other. (*See* VALENCE.)

Linus Pauling

Pauling next investigated compounds that occur in living tissue, especially proteins. (*See* PROTEIN.) He worked on the structure of their molecules. For this work, he won the 1954 Nobel Prize for chemistry. He also won the Nobel Peace Prize in 1962. He won it for his efforts in trying to stop nations from building nuclear weapons. He is one of only a few people who have won two Nobel Prizes.

M.E./D.G.F.

PAVLOV, IVAN PETROVICH (1849-1936) Ivan Pavlov was a Russian physiologist best known for his work with conditioned reflexes. (*See* LEARNING AND MEMORY; REFLEX.) In the early 1900s, Pavlov performed experiments concerned with digestion in dogs. When a dog sees food (the stimulus), it produces saliva (the reflex, or response). Pavlov tried ringing a bell while giving food to a dog.

Ivan
Petrovich Pavlov

After a while, he found that the dog produced saliva when it heard the bell, even though no food was given. Pavlov called this response a conditioned reflex. He believed that conditioned reflexes were the basis of learning. However, most scientists today believe that the mechanism of learning is much more complicated than this. Pavlov won a Nobel Prize for his work in 1904.   M.E./D.G.F.

PAYLOAD *See* SPACE TRAVEL.

PCBs PCBs, or polychlorinated biphenyls, are a group of two hundred synthetic (human-made) compounds first manufactured in 1930. (*See* COMPOUND.) They are formed by substituting up to ten chlorine atoms for atoms of hydrogen in a hydrocarbon called biphenyl.

(*See* HYDROCARBON.) In the 1970s, PCBs were shown to be harmful to the environment. The United States Environmental Protection Agency (EPA) banned their use in 1979.

Up until 1979, PCBs were widely used in industry as coolants and insulators. They were also used to manufacture a large number of products, such as paints and glues. By the 1960s, some scientists began to worry about the effect PCBs might have on the environment. (*See* ENVIRONMENT.) Research showed that many factories were releasing PCBs into the environment in their waste water.

PCBs came to be found in large quantities in various animals, such as fish and ducks. The chemicals caused duck eggshells to become thin, allowing them to be crushed easily. PCBs were also believed to cause some fish to be unable to reproduce. Humans who drank PCB-polluted water or ate birds, fish, and other animals contaminated with PCBs also became contaminated. High levels of PCBs in pregnant women resulted in birth defects. Children contaminated with PCBs had behavioral problems. PCBs may also cause liver damage and other medical problems.   P.Q.F./J.E.P.

PEACH (pēch) The peach (*Prunus persica*) is a tree belonging to the rose family. (*See* ROSE FAMILY.) It is cultivated in temperate areas throughout the world. The tree is usually about 20 ft. [6 m] tall. It has alternate, thin, pointed leaves with toothed margins. The flowers are usually pink and grow in the axils. They have five petals and five sepals. There are three whorls of stamens surrounding a central pistil. (*See* FLOWER; LEAF.)

The peach fruit is a drupe. (*See* DRUPE.) It has a fuzzy skin and a single pitted seed in the center. The two main varieties of peaches are freestone and clingstone. Freestone peach-

The fruit of the peach tree can be eaten as a fresh fruit or made into jam or jelly. Most of the peaches in the United States are grown in California.

es have seeds that separate easily from the fleshy, edible part of the fruit. The seeds of clingstone peaches are more firmly attached.

The peach can be eaten as a fresh fruit, or it may be canned or made into jam or jelly. In the United States, the popularity of the peach is second only to that of the apple. The United States produces more peaches than the rest of the world combined. California leads the country in peach production. *See also* NECTARINE.   A.J.C./F.W.S.

PEA FAMILY The pea (pē) family, Leguminosae, includes more than seven thousand species of flowering plants that grow throughout the world. The leaves vary widely, but most are alternate and divided. (*See* LEAF.) The flowers also vary, but most are butterfly shaped. The seeds are always enclosed in a legume, or pod. (*See* LEGUME.) Most members of the family have small, bacteria-containing nodules on the roots. These bacteria change nitrogen in the air into a form that can be used by the plant as food. (*See* NITROGEN FIXATION.)

The pea plant (*Pisum sativum*) is a vine with pinnately compound leaves and tendrils. (*See* TENDRIL.) It produces seeds—peas—which grow in legumes.

The pea is one of the best vegetables in terms of food value. It provides almost as much protein as meat. It is also a good source of carbohydrates and vitamins A and C. Peas grown in gardens and used for canning or freezing usually grow on low, bushy vines that are about 3.3 ft. [1 m] long. Peas sold as dry peas usually grow on climbing vines that are about 5 ft. [1.5 m] long. Other members of the pea family include the alfalfa, bean, clover, lentil, licorice, mimosa, peanut, soybean, sweet pea, and wisteria.

A.J.C./M.H.S.

PEACOCK *See* PEAFOWL.

PEAFOWL (pē′faùl′) A peafowl is a bird that belongs to the family Phasianidae. It is more commonly known as the peacock, though technically, *peacock* is the name for just the male peafowl. The female is called a peahen. There are three species of peafowl. One is native to India. Another is native to southeast Asia. A very rare species lives in Africa.

The peacock has a beautiful train of feathers that he displays during the breeding season. The feathers of the train are just in front of the bird's true tail feathers. Peafowl make harsh and sometimes startling cries at night. The calls are often mistaken for those of a person in trouble. Peafowl are omnivorous. *See also* OMNIVORE.   S.R.G./L L.S.

PEANUT (pē′nut′) The peanut (*Arachis hypogaea*) is a low-growing, annual plant belonging to the pea family. (*See* ANNUAL PLANT; PEA FAMILY.) The plant reaches a height of about 30 in. [75 cm] and a width of about 48 in. [120 cm]. The plant has many small flowers which, when pollinated, die within a few hours. (*See* POLLINATION.) The flower is followed by a small stalk called a peg. As the peg grows, the stem begins to bend toward the ground. The peg grows into the ground, sometimes to a depth of 3 in. [8 cm]. It then grows

Peanuts grow in legumes on the underground stems of the peanut plant (above). Most of the peanuts grown in the United States are made into peanut butter. They are also roasted and eaten. The peanut is almost 50 percent oil. Peanut oil is used for cooking and as a lubricant and a base for soap. Today, nearly all peanuts are harvested by machines. The machines lift the legumes out of the ground (below).

an underground legume. (*See* LEGUME.) The legume usually contains two seeds, but it may contain as many as five. It is these seeds that are called peanuts.

The peanut is almost 50 percent oil. In most countries, peanuts are cultivated for this oil. It is a popular cooking oil, a lubricant, and a base for soap. Once the oil has been removed, the pulpy remains can be used as a high-protein feed for livestock.

Peanuts have more protein, minerals, and vitamins than meat. Most of the peanuts grown in the United States are processed into peanut butter. They also are roasted and eaten or cooked into a variety of foods. *See also* CARVER, GEORGE WASHINGTON.   A.J.C./F.W.S.

PEAR (par) The pear is a tasty, fleshy fruit that grows on a large tree belonging to the rose family. (*See* ROSE FAMILY.) The common pear tree (*Pyrus communis*) reaches a height of 50 ft. [15 m] and may live for more than seventy-five years. It has alternate, oval leaves with toothed margins. (*See* LEAF.) White flowers grow in clusters of up to twelve blossoms. Each cluster produces one cone-shaped fruit with a smooth skin that may be yellow, red, or brown in color. The pear has a central core with as many as ten seeds. The fruit itself contains many tiny, hardened structures called grit cells. These grit cells give the pear a slightly sandy texture.

More than 95 percent of the pears produced in the United States are grown along the west coast. Pears are eaten as fresh fruit. They also may be canned, dried, or processed into fruit drinks. Pears contain large amounts of carbohydrates, vitamins, and minerals. Their popularity in the United States is exceeded only by that of the apple and the peach.

A.J.C./F.W.S.

PEARL (pərl) The pearl is a gem that forms inside the shell of certain mollusks, especially oysters. (*See* MOLLUSCA; OYSTER.) The inner layer of a mollusk shell consists of a very smooth and shiny material called nacre or mother-of-pearl. The substance is a form of calcium carbonate. It is secreted (produced) by the outer skin of the animal. This outer skin is called the mantle. Grains of sand and other foreign bodies often get inside the shell and cause irritation. The animal then responds by secreting more nacre around the object and forming a little, shiny ball. This ball is the pearl.

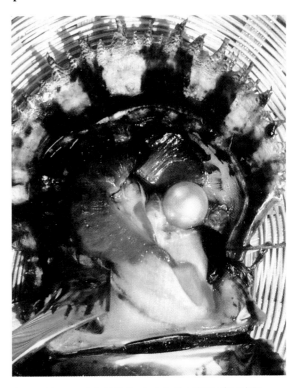

A pearl is a gem that forms inside the shell of certain mollusks, especially oysters, such as the one above. A pearl is formed when sand or another substance gets inside the shell and causes irritation. The mollusk forms a pearl around the substance.

Several kinds of mollusks make pearls. The pearl has the same luster and color as the lining of the shell of the mollusk that produced it. However, few pearl-forming mollusks make the nacre that is necessary to produce pearls that are considered especially valuable. The most highly valued pearls come from a few species of oysters found in tropical seas. These oysters are called pearl oysters. Pearl formation in these animals is usually triggered by a tiny parasitic worm that burrows into the mantle.

Pearl oysters are collected by divers in some parts of the Pacific Ocean. Natural pearls are very valuable for use in jewelry. However, most pearls made into jewelry today are cultured pearls. These are obtained by placing little pieces of nacre inside the oysters and waiting for the pearls to grow. When the oyster is seven years old, its shell is opened. There is a valuable pearl in about one out of every twenty such oysters opened.

J.J.A./C.S.H.

PEARY, ROBERT EDWIN (1856-1920) Robert Edwin Peary was an explorer who led the first expedition to reach the north pole. Peary was born in Cresson, Pennsylvania. He graduated from Bowdoin College in Maine. In 1881, Peary joined the U.S. Navy. He spent the next several years in Nicaragua, a country in Central America, surveying (measuring) land for a planned canal. The canal would join the Atlantic and Pacific oceans. This canal was later built through Panama, another country in Central America.

In the late 1880s, Peary made the first of several trips to the arctic region. Accompanied by explorer Matthew Henson, Peary traveled over Greenland, an island in the arctic region. (*See* HENSON, MATTHEW.) This trip took them farther into the arctic wilderness than people of European or African descent had been before. Peary returned to the arctic in 1891, accompanied by his wife and a doc-

tor, Frederick Cook. This time, Peary and his group traveled to northeastern Greenland. He returned with proof that Greenland was, in fact, an island.

Peary began his attempts to reach the north pole in 1893. He tried to establish routes to the pole both from Greenland and from Ellesmere Island, a Canadian island near Greenland. In 1905, he led an expedition that reached a latitude just beyond 87° north. (*See* LATITUDE AND LONGITUDE.) This was the closest that anyone had gotten to the north pole. The expedition was forced back by harsh weather. In 1909, Peary set out on his third attempt to reach the north pole. The expedition started with 24 men, 19 sleds, and 133 dogs. As supplies were used up, Peary sent the empty sleds back to the expedition's starting point. The party was gradually reduced to Peary, Henson, and four Eskimos. They reached the north pole on April 6, 1909.

The doctor on Peary's 1891 expedition, Frederick Cook, said that he had reached the north pole one year before Peary did. However, his claim was eventually disproved. The accuracy of Peary's claim of having reached the north pole was investigated by the National Geographic Society in the late 1980s. In 1990, the society stated that photographs supported Peary's claim. Peary wrote several books about his expeditions, including *Northward Over the Great Ice*, *The North Pole*, and *Secrets of Polar Travel*. A portion of northern Greenland is named Peary Land in his honor.

P.Q.F./L.W.

PEAT (pēt) Peat is partially decayed plant matter that has collected in marshes and swamps over a long period of time. It is generally the first stage in the formation of coal. (*See* COAL.) Dried peat is used mainly for fuel in places where coal and oil are scarce. Dried peat varies from a light yellow-brown substance resembling tangled hay to a denser mass of dark brown substance resembling brown coal.

Peat forms in layers. The upper layers contain the remains of plants that rotted and dried in the shallow, acidic waters of a marsh or swamp. The layers are compressed by the weight of the water and each other. The lower layers contain about 90 percent water and look like mud when first removed.

Peat is found throughout the world. The Soviet Union, Canada, and Finland have the largest deposits of peat. In the United States, the largest peat deposits are in Minnesota. The Dismal Swamp in Virgina also has peat bogs (swamps). Workers dig and stack peat by hand in Ireland and some other countries. Large machines are generally used for this work in the United States, Canada, the Soviet Union, and other European countries.

Peat is dried by simply exposing it to the air for a period of time. Dried peat is used as fuel to heat houses in Ireland. In the Soviet Union, it is used as fuel in some electric power plants. The dark peat also is used as a fertilizer. The fluffy, brown peat is used as a packing material.

W.R.P./R.J.B.

PECCARY (pek′ə rē) The peccary is a piglike mammal that lives in the forests and desert scrublands of Central and South America, Mexico, and the southwestern United States. Peccaries make up the family Tayassuidae and are distantly related to the true pigs (family Suidae).

There are three species of peccaries: the collared peccary, or javelina, which lives in South America and as far north as the United States; the white-lipped peccary, which is found in Mexico and Central and South America; and the tagua, or Chacoan peccary,

Peat is partially decayed plant matter that has collected over time in marshes and swamps. In some areas, such as the one in Ireland at left, peat is cut from the ground, left out in the air to dry, and then used as fuel.

Peccaries are piglike mammals that are native to Central and South America, Mexico, and the southwestern United States. Although they are ordinarily timid, peccaries will fight savagely when cornered or to protect their young.

which lives in Paraguay, Bolivia, and Argentina in South America.

Peccaries look like slender, active pigs. They can grow 30 in. [76 cm] tall and are covered with coarse, grizzled, blackish gray fur. Peccaries are rooting animals. They dig in the ground for roots to eat. They live in herds that can range in size from a few peccaries to several hundred. Peccaries are shy animals but fight viciously when cornered. The jaguar is their most dangerous natural enemy. Peccaries are hunted by people for their skin, which is used to make jackets and gloves.

W.R.P./J.J.M.

PECTIN (pek′tən) Pectin is a white substance found between the cell walls of many fruits. It is a complex carbohydrate made up of sugar molecules. (*See* CARBOHYDRATE.) Pectin forms a network of fibers when some fruits are cooked to be made into jelly. Pectin allows the fruit juices to jell, or thicken.

The amount of pectin in fruit depends upon the kind and ripeness of fruit. Some fruits are high in pectin. These include apples, blackberries, cranberries, gooseberries, logan-berries, grapes, currants, crab apples, and plums.

Commercial pectins are made by concentrating certain fruit juices. When jams are made from fruits low in natural pectin, commercial pectins are added. Peaches, pineapples, and strawberries are examples of fruits low in pectin.

W.R.P./M.H.S.

PECTORALIS MAJOR (pek′tə ral′əs ma′jər) The pectoralis major is the large muscle that covers most of the front of the chest. It originates at the ribs, sternum (breastbone), and clavicle (collarbone). The pectoralis major extends across the chest and is attached by a tendon to the humerus (the bone of the upper arm). The muscle is responsible for many of the arm's movements. It can pull the arm toward the side of the body or swing it forward in front of the chest.

The pectoralis minor is a smaller muscle that is underneath the pectoralis major. It originates at the ribs and is attached to the scapula (shoulder blade). This muscle is used to move the shoulder forward and downward. *See also* BONE; MUSCLE; TENDON. D.M.H.W./J.J.F.

PEKING MAN *See* HUMAN BEING.

PELICAN (pel'i kən) The pelican is a large bird that belongs to the family Pelecanidae. There are seven species in the world, but only two species—the brown pelican and the American white pelican—are common in North America. The brown pelican lives along the seashores of western and southeastern North America. The American white pelican winters in those areas, but it nests beside freshwater lakes of western and central North America.

Pelicans are large, fish-eating water birds with enormous pouched beaks. The pouches are not used to carry the birds' catch, but some species use them as fishing "nets." Pelicans feed their young by passing partly digested food back into the pouch. The young pelicans reach their heads into the pouches to get the food.

Pelicans grow about 45 in. [112 cm] long. They have webbed feet, a long neck, and a long, broad bill that is used to catch fish, the pelican's main food. Brown pelicans often dive from heights of 33 ft. [10 m] into the water to catch fish. S.R.G./L.L.S.

PELVIS (pel'vəs) The pelvis is a structure made of several bones that are fused together to support the lower abdomen and protect the internal organs. The pelvis has two halves called *ossa coxae,* or hipbones. Each hipbone is made up of three smaller bones: the ilium, ischium, and pubis. The hipbones are fused in front, and each side is attached to the sacrum (bottom bones of the spine) in the back. (*See* VERTEBRAE.) The ilium is the flat, blade-shaped bone that can be felt as the bone at the hip. The ischium supports the weight of the upper body when a person is sitting. The two pubis bones form an arch in front.

The spine, or backbone, rises from the top of the pelvis. The femurs (thighbones) are connected to the lower pelvis by ball-and-socket joints. (*See* FEMUR; JOINT.) These joints are very strong because they must support the weight of the upper part of the body when a person stands. There are many large, strong muscles leading from the pelvis to each femur.

A woman's pelvis is broader and more flared than a man's. This provides extra support during pregnancy for the uterus and the unborn baby. The central cavity of the pelvis is also larger in the woman so that the baby can pass through it during birth. *See also* BONE; SKELETON. A.J.C./J.J.F.; M.H.M.

PENDULUM (pen'jə ləm) A pendulum is a body that hangs from a fixed point and is free to swing. A simple pendulum consists of a heavy mass called a bob on the end of a lightweight cord or rod. If the cord or rod is not light, the pendulum is called a compound pendulum.

If a pendulum is held to one side and released, it swings down to the vertical (straight up-and-down) position. It continues moving away from the vertical and slows down until it stops. It then swings back the other way. It stops when it reaches the point at which it was released. The cycle then starts again. This movement of the pendulum is called oscillation. (*See* OSCILLATION.) A single oscillation consists of the pendulum's movement from its point of release and back one time.

The time it takes to complete one oscillation is called the period of oscillation. For small oscillations, the period depends only on the length of the rod or cord. It does not depend on the mass of the bob, nor does it depend on the angle through which the pendulum swings.

Pendulums are often used for timing in clocks, because the time it takes for a pendulum to complete each swing is the same.

The time that it takes for a pendulum to complete each swing is the same. Because of this, pendulums are used for timing in clocks. Christian Huygens, a Dutch scientist, invented the first clock with a pendulum in 1657. *See also* FOUCAULT PENDULUM. M.E./R.W.L.

PENGUIN (pen′gwən) Penguins are sixteen species of seabirds that belong to the order Sphenisciformes. Their wings have evolved into flippers. As a result, they cannot fly, but they are excellent swimmers. All penguins live in the southern hemisphere, mostly at the edge of Antarctica. Penguin colonies, or rookeries, are found where there are cold water currents, as far north as the Galapagos Islands, a group of Pacific Ocean islands near the equator. A single rookery may contain more than a million penguins.

All penguins walk in an upright position. Because they have stout bodies and such short legs, they walk with a waddling motion. A penguin's body is covered with a thick layer of short feathers that are white on the bird's belly and black or dark blue on its back. These feathers are waterproof and have tiny air spaces that help keep the bird warm. Penguins spend much of their time in icy waters, swimming or looking for food. Their diet consists mostly of fish and squid.

The emperor penguin (*Aptenodytes forsteri*) is the largest penguin. It is about 4 ft. [1.2 m] tall. *See also* BIRD. A.J.C./L.L.S.

Penguins live in cold areas of the southern hemisphere. Because their wings have evolved into flippers, they cannot fly. Penguins often play by sliding on their bellies over the snow or ice.

PENICILLIN (pen'ə sil'ən) Penicillin is a powerful antibiotic. (*See* ANTIBIOTIC.) It is made by molds belonging to the genus *Penicillium.* Penicillin was discovered in 1928 by Alexander Fleming. In 1940, Howard Florey and Ernst Chain purified penicillin for use in medicine. (*See* CHAIN, ERNST BORIS; FLEMING, SIR ALEXANDER; FLOREY, HOWARD WALTER; MOLD.) The effectiveness of the drug caused an interest that led to the development of many drugs known as antibiotics.

At first, penicillin could be made only in small amounts. Later, a method was developed in which large amounts of the mold were grown in tanks. Soon, more productive strains of penicillin were found. The strains used by manufacturers today produce almost five thousand times as much penicillin as those first used by researchers. Hundreds of tons of penicillin are made every year in the United States.

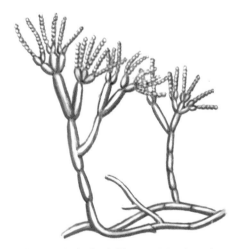

A magnified part of a Penicillium mold colony shows the spores (the green circular structures) that reproduce the mold.

Not all harmful microorganisms are destroyed by penicillin. However, most of the bacteria that cause common infections, such as *Streptococcus* and *Staphylococcus,* are very sensitive to penicillin. (*See* BACTERIA; MICROORGANISM.)

Penicillin is the least poisonous antibiotic available, though a few people are allergic to it. For these people, even a tiny amount of the drug can cause a serious reaction. (*See* ALLERGY.)

Many bacteria are resistant—that is, they can grow even when an antibiotic is present. For example, though the proper dosage of penicillin will kill most *Staphylococci,* some strains resist penicillin and require different antibiotics for treatment.   J.J.A./J.J.F.; M.H.M.

PENNSYLVANIAN PERIOD (pen'səl vā'-nyen pir'ē əd) The Pennsylvanian period is the division of the Paleozoic era in the earth's history that began about 325 million years ago. It lasted about 45 million years and is the second half of the Carboniferous period. (*See* CARBONIFEROUS PERIOD; PALEOZOIC ERA.)

In North America today, rocks of the Pennsylvanian period contain vast amounts of coal, natural gas, and petroleum (oil). This is because during the Pennsylvanian period, forests of huge ferns grew in the swampy soil. Over time, these plants died and decayed, and layers of soil and rock piled on top of them. After many years, the decayed plants were pressed into coal, petroleum, or natural gas. (*See* COAL; NATURAL GAS; PETROLEUM.)

During the Pennsylvanian period, hundreds of insect species, including giant cockroaches, thrived. Amphibians and sea life flourished. Reptiles made their first appearance during the Pennsylvanian period. *See also* GEOLOGICAL TIME SCALE.   J.M.C./W.R.S.

PEONY (pē'ə nē) The peony is a plant with large, attractive flowers. Peonies make up the peony family, Paeoniaceae. In early spring, peonies have soft or woody stems. The cluster of leafy shoots—red and bright green in

The peony plant blooms with large, beautiful flowers in late spring or early summer. The blossoms are usually white, pink, or red.

appearance—creates a striking effect a few weeks before the flowers appear in late spring or early summer. The flower blossoms are usually white, pink, or red. Peonies grow 3 to 4 ft. [90 to 120 cm] high. They are found throughout the world.

Many of the cultivated peonies found in the United States are offsprings of two species—the common peony of southern Europe and the Chinese peony. Peonies are hardy plants that live a long time. *See also* PERENNIAL PLANT.   W.R.P./M.H.S.

PEPPER FAMILY The pepper (pep′ər) family, Piperaceae, includes ten genera (plural of *genus*) with more than 1,500 species of dicotyledonous flowering plants. (*See* DICOTYLEDON.) The family includes herbaceous plants, shrubs, vines, and trees, most of which grow in tropical areas. (*See* HERBACEOUS PLANT.) They have alternate, simple leaves. The flowers do not have sepals or petals. They grow in dense spikes. (*See* INFLORESCENCE; LEAF.) Most of the plants are monoecious, with both male flowers and female flowers on the same plant.

The most important member of the pepper family is the black pepper plant, *Piper nigrum*. It is a perennial climbing plant that produces aerial roots. (*See* PERENNIAL PLANT; ROOT.) It may reach a length of 33 ft. [10 m]. It produces small berries called peppercorns that turn from green to red as they mature. The peppercorns are usually harvested at maturity, cleaned, and dried. The peppercorns become black as they dry. They can then be ground, sifted, and sold as the spice called black pepper. White pepper comes from the same plant, but the husk is removed from the peppercorn before it is ground.

These peppercorns are dried berries of the black pepper plant. Once ground and sifted, they are sold as black pepper, one of the world's most widely used spices.

Red pepper and garden peppers come from plants belonging to genus *Capsicum* of the nightshade family. (*See* NIGHTSHADE FAMILY.) They are not related to the pepper family.   A.J.C./M.H.S.

PERCENT (pər sent′) Percent is a rate or proportion per hundred. It comes from the

Latin phrase *per centum,* meaning "by the hundred." For example, the statement, "Thirty percent of the students at this school are wearing red sweaters" means that out of every 100 students in the school, 30 of them are wearing red sweaters. In other words, 30 hundredths of the students are wearing red sweaters. Hundredths may be expressed as common fractions, such as $^{30}/_{100}$; as decimal fractions, 0.30; or as percent, 30 percent. Each of these figures represents a ratio of 30 compared to 100. The symbol for percent is %.

Numbers greater than a whole ($^{100}/_{100}$) also can be expressed as percents. To say something has increased to 300 percent means it is three times as large as it was.

To change a decimal fraction to a percent, the decimal fraction is multiplied by 100. This is done by moving the decimal point two places to the right and adding the percent sign. For example, 0.25 = 25%, 0.50 = 50%, and 0.4782 = 47.82%. To change a common fraction to a percent, the common fraction is first changed to a decimal fraction. For example, $^{1}/_{10}$ = 0.10 = 10%.

Such operations can be reversed. For example, 50% = 0.50 = ½. The percent is divided by 100 by moving the decimal point two places to the left and dropping the percent sign. The decimal fraction may then be changed to a common fraction.

Percents are used in everyday life. Bankers use percents to figure interest on savings accounts. In baseball, team standings and batting averages are based on percents. Scientists often show the results of their observations and experiments with percents. *See also* FRACTION; RATIO.　　　　J.J.A./S.P.A.; R.J.S.

PERCEPTION (pər sep′shən) Perception is the process by which a person or animal makes sense out of the things in its environment. The world consists of various kinds of physical energy. Knowledge of the world comes through the sense organs. For example, the ears sense certain types of mechanical vibrations (sound) in the air. The eyes sense certain wavelengths of electromagnetic energy (light). (*See* EAR; EYE AND VISION; SENSE.)

The sense organs change the various kinds of energy into nerve impulses. These impulses go to the brain. (*See* NERVOUS SYSTEM.) Through the process of perception, the patterns of energies become known as objects and events. In this process, the sense organs and the brain transform physical energy into information.

There are three different levels of perception: detection, recognition, and discrimination. Detection is the ability to sense that one is being stimulated by some form of energy. For example, a sound may be so slight that a person can hardly hear it. Recognition is being able to identify a particular pattern of stimulation, such as being able to tell that a particular sound is a tone from a piano. Discrimination is being able to perceive patterns of stimulation as different, such as differences between two similar musical tones. *See also* OPTICAL ILLUSION; PSYCHOLOGY.

J.J.A./J.J.F.

PERCH (pərch) A perch is a freshwater fish that belongs to the family Percidae. North American fish included in the perch family are the darters, walleye, and yellow perch. The yellow perch is very common in lakes and rivers throughout North America. It often is called simply a perch. The yellow perch ranges between 7 and 16 in. [18 and 40 cm] in length. Its body is green along the top and yellowish on the belly and has orange stripes

Also, the heat of buildings may thaw permafrost, causing buildings to sink up to 1 ft. [0.3 m] or more.   C.C./J.E.P.

PERMIAN PERIOD (pər′mē ən pir′ē əd) The Permian period is the time in the earth's history that began about 280 million years ago and lasted about 55 million years. It is the last division of the Paleozoic era. (*See* PALEOZOIC ERA.)

At the beginning of the Permian period, the southern continents were mostly covered with ice. At the same time, the climate of northern continents remained warm and dry. Significant effects of continental drift are thought to have occurred during the Permian period. (*See* CONTINENTAL DRIFT.)

Conifers, the first seed plants, appeared during the Permian period. Fish, amphibians, and reptiles flourished. In the oceans, there were many ammonites and brachiopods. Trilobites died out. (*See* AMMONITE; BRACHIOPOD; TRILOBITE.)

Sedimentary rock containing copper formed during this time in parts of Texas and Oklahoma in the United States and in Germany. (*See* SEDIMENTARY ROCK.) Great folding also occurred at this time during the formation of the Ural Mountains in the western Soviet Union and the Appalachian Mountains in the eastern United States. *See also* FOLDING; GEOLOGICAL TIME SCALE.   J.M.C./W.R.S.

PERPETUAL MOTION (pər pech′ə wəl mō′shən) Perpetual motion is motion that goes on forever. Throughout history, people have tried to build perpetual motion machines. These machines were supposed to operate indefinitely. However, all attempts at making such machines have failed.

By the 1850s, scientists had discovered two reasons why perpetual motion machines cannot be invented. These reasons are embodied in two very important laws of physics: the first and second laws of thermodynamics. (*See* THERMODYNAMICS.)

This is a view of the Shenandoah Valley in the Appalachian mountain range of the eastern United States. The Appalachians formed during the Permian period.

The first law of thermodynamics says that energy can be neither created nor destroyed. This law is also called the law of conservation of energy. (*See* ENERGY.) A perpetual motion machine that attempts to break this law is called a perpetual motion machine of the first kind. One example consists of a wheel with spokes. Each spoke has a ball that can move along it between the rim and the hub. When the spoke is near the bottom of the wheel, the ball can fall to the rim of the wheel. As the wheel keeps turning, the ball should fall back to the hub (middle of the wheel). When the wheel moves around a little more, the ball should fall back to the rim again. The force of it hitting the rim is supposed to keep the wheel turning. However, the ball loses energy as it hits the rim, and friction occurs as the ball rolls down the spoke. (*See* FRICTION.) The wheel soon stops.

The second law of thermodynamics states that heat cannot flow from a colder body to a hotter one without adding more energy than is produced. Perpetual motion machines that do not work because they break the second law of thermodynamics are called perpetual motion machines of the second kind. Machines that attempt to turn heat into other forms of energy with complete efficiency violate this law. (*See* EFFICIENCY.)

Recently, experiments in superconductivity have come close to achieving perpetual motion. In superconductivity, certain substances lose their electrical resistance at very low temperatures. (*See* SUPERCONDUCTIVITY.) This means that an electric current can flow through the substance forever. However, energy is needed to keep the substance cold. For this reason, machines that employ superconductivity do not qualify as perpetual motion machines. M.E./J.T.

PERSPECTIVE (pər spek′tiv) Perspective is a way of showing a solid object on flat paper. A solid object has three dimensions: length, width, and depth. A surface, such as the top of a piece of paper, has only two dimensions. The third dimension of an object is represented by perspective.

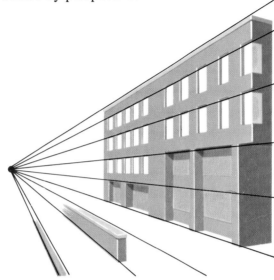

A perspective drawing is one in which everything appears at the size it would be if viewed in depth by an observer. To give the impression of depth in this picture, the artist selects a point on the horizon where the lines of the building converge—the vanishing point. If the artist added other buildings to the drawing, their vanishing points would be different.

Any object appears to become smaller as we move away from it. This is called linear perspective. For example, the farther side of a cube seems smaller than the nearer side. The two lines that join the two sides do not seem parallel. They are said to converge (come together) at a point on the horizon. This point is called the vanishing point. Artists use the vanishing point to show perspective in drawings. M.E./S.S.B.

PESTICIDE (pes′tə sīd′) A pesticide is a chemical that is used to kill pests. A pest may be an animal, plant, protozoan, fungus, bacterium, alga, or virus. Some pests spread disease.

Others eat or cause other damage to crops and other desirable plants. Some pests are parasites that harm livestock, pets, and human beings. (*See* PARASITE.)

Pesticides that kill insects are called insecticides. (*See* INSECTICIDE.) Pesticides that kill fungi (plural of *fungus*) are called fungicides. (*See* FUNGICIDE.) Pesticides that kill weeds or other plants are called herbicides. (*See* HERBICIDE.) Rats and other rodent pests are often controlled with anticoagulants. These chemicals keep the rodent's blood from clotting so that the animal bleeds to death from even the tiniest scratch. Pheromones are also used as pesticides. Pheromones are chemicals that are used to attract pests, such as by scent, into a trap, where the pests are captured or killed. (*See* PHEROMONE.) Various poisons have been used to control pests. However, these poisons often have affected other organisms as well, including humans. Scientists are constantly working on new chemicals that will affect only specific, targeted pests.

Pesticides are used by farmers to kill pests that harm crops (above). This practice can be dangerous, however. Traces of the pesticides may remain on crops that people eat. In addition, some pesticides may get into water that may be used as drinking water. Pesticides also are frequently used around houses to kill such pests as ants, roaches, and termites (below). Pesticides are poisonous chemicals that must only be used as recommended by their manufacturers.

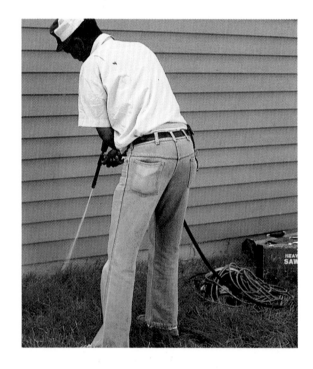

Because they are poisonous, pesticides must be handled very carefully. It is important to dispose of pesticide containers properly, such as at a hazardous waste collection center. The containers should not be rinsed and reused. Rinsing allows the pesticide to enter the sewer system. Also, some pesticide may remain in the container even after rinsing.

The use of pesticides in agriculture has been criticized because residues (traces) of pesticide may remain on crops that are later eaten by humans. (*See* AGRICULTURE.) Some pesticide may seep into groundwater or be washed by rain into bodies of water. (*See* GROUNDWATER.) This is dangerous to humans and other animals because this water may be used as drinking water.

Some pesticides are short lasting. This means they remain poisonous just long enough to kill the pest. However, some pesticides remain poisonous for years. They may be passed along in the food chain, becoming more concentrated—and thus, more harmful —as they do so. (*See* FOOD CHAIN.)

In many cases, a pest becomes resistant to a certain pesticide after repeated exposure. This means that the pesticide can no longer kill the pest. For example, some rats and boll weevils have become resistant to certain pesticides. When this happens, the pest population may increase rapidly, often becoming a greater problem than before.

Because of these concerns, many farmers have started using a system called integrated pest management (IPM). In IPM, a variety of methods are used to control pests, so pesticide use is decreased. One of these methods is called biological control. In biological control, natural enemies are used to fight off pests. *See also* BIOLOGICAL CONTROL.

A.J.C.; C.C./R.J.B.; J.E.P.

PETAL (pet′əl) The petal is the part of a flower that is usually brightly colored and leaf-like in shape. Its main function is to attract insects and birds to the flower for pollination. (*See* POLLINATION.) Most monocotyledons

The petals of these mountain laurel flowers are fused.

have petals in multiples of three. Most dicotyledons have petals in multiples of four or five (*See* DICOTYLEDON; MONOCOTYLEDON.) Sometimes, the petals may be fused to form a cup- or tube-like corolla. *See also* FLOWER; MIMICRY.

A.J.C./M.H.S.

PETREL (pe′trəl) Petrels are small seabirds that belong to the order Procellarüformes. There are several species of petrels found off the coasts of North America.

Petrels are long-winged, strong-flying birds. They are usually brown and white. All petrels have tubelike nostrils on the top of the beak. Petrels eat fish, shrimp, and microscopic organisms called plankton. The group of petrels known as storm-petrels often follow ships at sea, eating wastes that are thrown overboard. *See also* BIRD.

S.R.G./L.L.S.

Petrified Forest National Park in Arizona contains the world's most famous collection of fossilized wood. The trees there grew about 150 million years ago. After they died, they were transformed into colorful fossils.

PETRIFIED FOREST A petrified (pe′trə-fīd) forest is a forest of trees that have been fossilized. (*See* FOSSIL.) The fossilization process usually begins when the plants are rapidly buried by volcanic ash, mud, or sand. Water containing minerals seeps through the debris into the buried plants. There, the silica or calcium carbonate in the water replaces the decaying plant cells. The result is an exact duplicate of the original plant. Plants fossilized in this way are sometimes the only record of species that flourished on earth for a very short period of time.

In a petrified forest, the trees are no longer standing. Instead, many petrified logs lie in scattered positions. They have been disturbed by erosion. (*See* EROSION.) The Petrified Forest National Park in Arizona contains the largest and most colorful collection of petrified plants in the world. The trees probably grew about 150 million years ago. Other petrified forests in the United States are found in New York and Wyoming. *See also* PALEOBOTANY.

J.M.C./W.R.S.

PETROLEUM (pə trō′lē əm) Petroleum is a thick, black liquid found usually in pools beneath the earth's surface. It is one of the most valuable substances found in the earth's crust. Petroleum consists of a mixture of oils from which gasoline, fuel oils, lubricating oils, and other substances are produced. Petroleum is sometimes called "black gold" because it is so valuable to human beings. Petroleum directly from the earth is also referred to as crude oil.

Formation of petroleum The word *petroleum*, meaning "rock oil," comes from the Greek. Petroleum formed from the decayed remains of organisms that lived in shallow seas millions of years ago. These remains were buried in clay or silt brought down by rivers and were decomposed into simple hydrocarbons by bacteria. (*See* DECOMPOSITION.) Eventually, the clay or silt were buried and enclosed by permeable rocks (porous rocks through which liquids can flow), such as sandstone or limestone. The pressure of these rocks turned the clay or silt into another kind of rock called shale. The simple compounds were changed by pressure into long-chain hydrocarbon oils. (*See* COMPOUND; HYDROCARBON; SHALE.) The oil was squeezed out of the shale and flowed into the permeable rocks. Experts believe that the differences between one kind of petroleum and another come from differences in temperature, pressure, and other conditions, instead of differences in the living creatures from which they were formed.

Where petroleum is found For petroleum to be extracted (removed), it must have collected in reservoirs in the earth's crust. Also, the permeable rocks in which it collected must have been sealed to prevent the petroleum from leaking away. Oil floats on water, and, usually, collects in structures that are sealed on top. The impermeable cap rock that seals an underground reservoir of petroleum is usually shale or rock salt. (*See* ROCK SALT.)

The most common reservoir for petroleum is an anticline. This is an upfold of rocks that forms an underground dome or ridge. (*See* ANTICLINE.) Another structure where petroleum is sometimes found is a salt dome. A salt dome is a body of salt that has been forced up, breaking apart and tilting the layers of rock below it and raising those above it into a dome. Petroleum collects in the rocks above the salt dome.

Another type of reservoir can occur when rocks are tilted and then faulted, so that an impermeable shale or other kind of rock is brought next to the permeable one. (*See* FAULT.) In this way, the oil is sealed on the underside of the fault.

Prospecting for petroleum Possible reservoirs containing petroleum are found by geologists and geophysicists. (*See* GEOLOGY; GEOPHYSICS.) Geologists study surface rocks and map their findings. This increases their knowledge about the structures beneath the ground. The structures can be measured more accurately by geophysicists, who use the principles of seismology. (*See* SEISMOLOGY.) Seismological methods involve making small explosions in the ground and measuring the shock waves that pass through the earth's crust. The shock waves are deflected at boundaries between different types of rock. The type and structure of the rock can be established by noting the time the shock waves take to travel to various places around the explosion.

Another method of prospecting for petroleum involves measuring the force of gravity at various places. For example, when a salt dome lies beneath the earth's surface, the force of gravity at the surface is slightly reduced. (*See* GRAVITY.)

Despite these sophisticated methods, geophysicists can establish only that a reservoir of petroleum may exist. The only way to find out whether the reservoir actually contains petroleum is to drill a hole. (*See* PROSPECTING.)

Petroleum is removed from beneath the earth's surface using pumps like this one in Utah.

Extracting petroleum Early uses for petroleum included lighting, treating roads, waterproofing, and medicine. In those times, people did not drill for oil but used the oils that leaked naturally out of the surface of the earth. Later, they drilled shallow holes by hand. The first mechanical drilling for oil was done by Edwin Drake in Pennsylvania in 1859. He used a steam engine. Early drilling was done by percussion (breaking up the rock by hammering).

Much drilling today is performed with a rotating (turning) shaft. Different types of bits (the drilling mechanism at the end of the shaft) are used, depending on the hardness of the rock that has to be drilled through. (*See* DRILLING.) The bits break the rocks to fragments, which are washed out with water and soft clay. When geologists want to study the rocks being drilled, a coring bit is used. Coring bits have diamonds around the edges to cut through the rock. They also have a hollow center to hold the core. The core is removed occasionally for examination.

Usually, petroleum is found floating on salty water. Often a layer of natural gas is found on top of the petroleum. This natural gas consists mostly of methane. (*See* METHANE; NATURAL GAS.) Often, it is the only useful substance obtained from drilling. Petroleum may be absent or nearly so.

If a reservoir is found, it may be under great pressure. When the drilling reaches the reservoir, the petroleum may burst out in what is called a gusher. Gushers are prevented whenever possible because they are wasteful and cause pollution.

When the pressure falls, petroleum is pumped out of the reservoir. The final stage is to flush out any remaining oil with water. Still, one-fifth to more than one-half of the petroleum may be left behind. It clings to the walls of small holes in the rock. The amount left behind depends on the size of the holes. The smaller the hole, the more petroleum is lost.

Since World War II (1939-1945), offshore drilling, or drilling below the ocean floor off the coast, has proved very productive. Most offshore drilling in the United States is done in the Pacific Ocean off the coast of California and in the Gulf of Mexico off the coasts of Louisiana and Texas.

After the petroleum has been taken out, it is taken by pipeline, truck, rail, or ship to a refinery. There, the petroleum is separated and changed into a number of useful products.

Chemistry of petroleum Petroleum consists of compounds of carbon and hydrogen, called hydrocarbons. (*See* HYDROCARBON.) Petroleum also contains small amounts of oxygen, nitrogen, and sulfur. The main compounds of petroleum are paraffins. These compounds have carbon atoms joined into chains by single bonds. Petroleum usually has small amounts of olefins. Olefins are like the paraffins except that some of the carbon atoms have two bonds between them and, therefore, fewer hydrogen atoms. (*See* OLEFIN.)

Refining petroleum Petroleum is first heated (distilled) in a furnace, and the gases are passed into a chimney called a fractionating column. (*See* DISTILLATION.) The column is hot at the bottom and gets cooler toward the top. When petroleum boils, the lighter substances in the petroleum travel up the fractionating column. Then they condense into liquids. (*See* CONDENSATION.) These liquids are collected in vessels called bubble cap trays, which are placed at intervals up the column. The collected liquids are called fractions. The lightest fractions supply gasoline. Increasingly heavy

Rigs for offshore drilling of petroleum are built on tall stilts (above). Once extracted, petroleum may be taken by a pipeline (below) to a refinery.

After petroleum has been removed from the earth, it is transported to a refinery (above left). There, the petroleum is separated and changed into a number of products, including gasoline, diesel oil, and lubricating oil. Large tanker trucks, such as the one above right, deliver gasoline to service stations. The service stations, in turn, supply the gasoline to automobiles, trucks, and other motorized vehicles.

fractions are used to make kerosene and fuel oil. The fuel oil cannot be separated simply by boiling in air, so residue is reheated in a vacuum, where the fractions boil at a much lower temperature. (*See* VACUUM.) This further boiling yields diesel oil, lubricating oil, asphalt, and paraffin wax.

The chief use of refined petroleum today is as gasoline or diesel oil for engines. Petroleum that is not refined does not yield lighter fractions that can be made into these products. To increase the supply of gasoline and diesel oil, the heavier fractions of petroleum are broken down into lighter ones by cracking. Cracking is performed by heating the heavier fractions under pressure, sometimes using a catalyst. (*See* CATALYST; CRACKING.)

Petroleum contains a wide range of compounds. Many more are made when it is refined. These compounds are the starting materials for the petrochemical industry. The petrochemical industry produces a wide range of plastics, fabrics, drugs, explosives, and other products.

Production of petroleum New reservoirs of petroleum are being tapped. Some of the most productive are in Alaska and the North Sea between Britain and mainland Europe.

Another new source of oil is oil shale. Oil can also be taken from tar sands. Because oil can be made from coal and hydrogen, coal deposits remain the most valuable source for future oil supplies. Coal is itself a source of energy because it burns. It does not, however, provide the many petrochemicals that are by-products of petroleum.

Scientists predict that the world's petroleum supply will be used early in the twenty-first century. Therefore, new sources of energy must be found. Whatever these new sources are, the diminishing of the petroleum supply will force us to make huge changes in our way of life. *See also* ENERGY.   J.J.A./J.M.; E.D.W.

PETROLOGY (pə träl′ə jē) Petrology is the study of rocks. This branch of geology deals with the formation, chemical composition, and structure of rocks. Petrologists also study the effect of erosion on rocks, as well as other ways in which rocks change. (*See* EROSION.) Petrography deals with the classification and description of rocks. *See also* GEOLOGY; ROCK.

J.M.C./W.R.S.

Petrologists study rocks, such as those in this collection of samples.

PEWEE (pē′wē′) The pewee is a small bird that belongs to the flycatcher family, Tyrannidae. It is mostly olive brown with white bars on its wings. The pewee grows to 5 in. [12 cm] long. There are two species of pewees that are common in North America. The eastern wood pewee lives in most areas east of the Missouri River. The western wood pewee lives in most areas west of the Missouri. Pewees live in wooded places and eat insects. *See also* BIRD.

S.R.G./L.L.S.

PEWTER (pyüt′ər) Pewter is an alloy consisting chiefly of tin, with small amounts of antimony and copper. (*See* ALLOY.) Pewter has a color similar to silver and a finish that may vary from dull to glossy.

Most pewter contains at least 90 percent tin, which is a very soft metal. Antimony and copper are added to give pewter hardness and strength. At one time, much pewter contained lead. However, lead dissolves in some foods and beverages contained in pewter ware,

Mugs (left), pitchers, and other utensils have been made of pewter, an alloy of tin and other metals, for hundreds of years.

forming poisonous substances. Lead also causes tarnishing. As a result, in the 1700s, people switched from pewter that contained lead to britannia metal —a pewter that contains copper instead of lead. This kind of pewter is most common today. Articles such as candlesticks, mugs, and pitchers are often made of pewter.

J.J.A./A.D.

PH Scientists use a pH number to show the strength of an acid or base. (*See* ACID; BASE.) The number is generally on a scale from 0 to 14. A pH lower than 7 indicates that the solution is an acid. A pH greater than 7 indicates that the solution is a base. Strong acids have lower pHs than weak acids. Strong bases have higher pHs than weak bases. A neutral solution is neither an acid or a base. It has a pH of 7.

A solution's pH is defined as the negative logarithm, to the base 10, of its hydrogen-ion concentration. This concentration is expressed in moles of hydrogen ions per liter of solution. (*See* IONS AND IONIZATION; LOGARITHM; MOLE

(UNIT); SOLUTION AND SOLUBILITY.) For example, a solution with a pH of 6 contains 10^{-6} (one-millionth) of a mole of hydrogen ions per liter.

Soil needs to have a suitable pH for plants to grow properly. For example, potatoes grow best in slightly acidic soil. A solution of ammonium sulfate is sometimes added to very acidic soil to lower the pH. Human skin, at about 6.5 pH, is slightly acidic. Ordinary hand soap is a base with a pH that is usually between 7 and 9. Some soap, shampoo, and skin products are chemically adjusted to be closer to the skin's natural pH.   J.J.A.; C.C./A.D.; J.E.P.

PHALANGE (fā′lanj′) Phalanges are the small bones in the fingers, thumbs, and toes of the human body. Each finger contains three phalanges, and each thumb has two. There are fourteen phalanges in the toes of a foot—three in each toe except the big toe, which has two. *See also* BONE.   W.R.P./J.J.F.

PHARMACOLOGY (fär′mə käl′ə jē) Pharmacology is the branch of science and medicine that studies the effects of drugs on organ-

Pharmacologists are scientists who study drugs and their effects on organisms.

isms. (*See* DRUG.) Pharmacology combines biology and chemistry in finding out how drugs change the workings of tissues and organs.

Pharmacology includes many specialized areas of study. Chemotherapy uses specific drugs to treat disease. Psychopharmacology studies drugs that affect behavior. Pharmacogenetics studies the effects of drugs on hereditary factors. Toxicology studies poisonous and potentially poisonous drugs. Pharmacy involves preparing and giving out appropriate drugs to treat diseases.   A.J.C./J.J.F.; M.H.M.

PHASE (fāz) *Phase* has several different meanings in science. In physics, *phase* refers to wave motions such as light and sound. If two waves have exactly the same intensity and frequency and are vibrating together exactly, they are said to be in phase. They can then make each other stronger. If they are completely out of phase, they can cancel each other out. (*See* BEAT; FREQUENCY.)

In chemistry, a mixture of water and ice is called a two-phase system. This is because there is a definite boundary between the water and the ice. Salt dissolved in water is a one-phase system. There is no boundary between the salt and the water.

In astronomy, the moon and other planets go through phases. As the moon goes around the earth, different parts of the moon are lit by the sun. The different appearances of the moon are called phases. In the same way, the planets Mercury and Venus, when viewed from earth, have different phases as they travel around the sun.   M.E./R.W.L.

PHEASANT (fez′ənt) The pheasant is a large bird that belongs to the family Phasianidae. Pheasants are characterized by long,

The male ring-necked pheasant has a white ring of feathers around its neck.

trailing tail feathers. The male is colorful, and the female is brown.

Pheasants are native to Asia, where there are many species. One species, the ring-necked pheasant, has been brought to the United States and Canada, where it has become established in the wild. The ring-necked pheasant is a popular game bird. Although the pheasant lives in many places, it does best in grassy fields. It feeds on grain, seeds, and fruits. The ring-necked pheasant received its name because the male bird has a white ring of feathers around its neck. Pheasants grow to about 28 in. [70 cm] long. *See also* BIRD.

S.R.G./L.L.S.

PHENOL (fē'nōl') Phenols are a group of organic (carbon-containing) chemical compounds. (*See* COMPOUND.) They contain one or more hydroxyl groups (OH^-) attached to a benzene ring. They are similar to alcohols. (*See* ALCOHOL; BENZENE.) Alcohols, however, usually have a hydroxyl group at-

tached to a chain of carbon atoms. Like alcohols, phenols combine with organic acids to form compounds called esters. (*See* ESTER.) Phenols can also act as weak acids. They form salts called phenates. In a phenate, the hydrogen atom in the hydroxyl group is replaced by a metal atom. (*See* ACID; SALTS.)

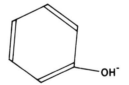

Phenols are a group of chemical compounds that contain one or more hydroxyl groups (OH^-) attached to a benzene ring.

Phenols are found in coal tar. (*See* COAL GAS.) They are used to make dyes, disinfectants, drugs, and plastics. *Phenol* is also the name given to the simplest phenol compound. Its formula is C_6H_5OH. It is also known as carbolic acid. Carbolic acid is obtained from coal tar but can also be made artificially. It is a strong antiseptic and is both poisonous and corrosive. *See also* ANTISEPTIC; CORROSION.

M.E./J.M.

Pheromones are special chemicals that are produced by animals and that make other animals of the same kind behave in a particular way. The moth above secretes pheromones that attract a mate, often over long distances.

PHEROMONE (fer′ə mōn′) Pheromones are special chemicals produced by animals that make other animals of the same kind behave in a particular way. They are one of the ways in which animals can communicate with one another. When a male cat marks out his territory by spraying trees and other objects with very strong-smelling urine, he is using a pheromone. It tells other male cats to keep away from his territory. This is an obvious example of a pheromone, because the odor is noticeable, even to humans.

Scientists have discovered other pheromones that are not obvious to humans. Moths produce pheromones that attract their mates. Ants use pheromones to mark food trails and to signal when to attack and when to flee. Worker bees mark the nest of their colony with pheromones to help bees who are returning from gathering food distinguish their nest from others. When it is time to mate, the queen bee secretes a pheromone that attracts the drones. (*See* BEE.)

When human beings enter adolescence, their perspiration takes on an odor. The production of the pheromones responsible for this odor is one of the changes in the chemistry of the body that takes place with sexual maturity. C.M./M.J.C.; C.R.N.

PHLEBITIS (fli bīt′əs) Phlebitis is an inflammation of the wall of a vein. (*See* INFLAMMATION; VEIN.) It usually occurs when part of the lining of a vein becomes damaged or diseased. The wall of the vein swells and becomes painful. If the vein is close to the skin, it may appear enlarged and reddened. Phlebitis is dangerous because blood tends to clot wherever the smooth wall of a blood vessel is damaged and roughened. This clot (or thrombus) may increase in size and may eventually block the vein. A blocked vein can create long-term circulatory problems in the area in which it is located. Additionally, a piece of the clot may break off and be carried in the bloodstream. A clot that has broken off and is being carried in the bloodstream is called an embolus. If an embolus carries bacteria with it, it will spread infection to various parts of the body. If the embolus settles in the heart, it can cause a heart attack.

Phlebitis can be treated with drugs that keep the blood from forming clots. If there is an infection, antibiotics may be used to kill the bacteria. (*See* ANTIBIOTIC.) In severe cases, a surgeon may have to remove the clot itself or a length of badly damaged vein. *See also* CIRCULATORY SYSTEM.　　D.M.H.W./J.J.F.; M.H.M.

PHLOEM (flō′əm′) Phloem is the food-carrying tissue found in the leaves, stems, and roots of vascular plants. (*See* VASCULAR PLANT.) Phloem takes sugar and other foods produced by photosynthesis from the leaves to all other parts of the plant. (*See* PHOTO-SYNTHESIS.)

The phloem of angiosperms is made up of tube-shaped cells arranged end to end. (*See* ANGIOSPERM.) There are small holes in the ends of the cells, so that there is a continuous tube for food transport. Each cell is called a sieve tube. It is living and has cytoplasm but has no nucleus. Next to each sieve tube is a nucleus-containing companion cell. The companion cell apparently controls the working of the sieve tube cell. (*See* CELL.) There are

usually fibers extending through the phloem for added strength. Fluids pass from one sieve tube to another through sieve plates—cell walls perforated with holes.

The phloem of dicotyledons is arranged in an orderly pattern. In woody plants, it is part of the inner bark. The phloem of monocotyledons is arranged in random bundles with the xylem throughout the stem. (*See* DICOTYLEDON; MONOCOTYLEDON; WOODY PLANT; XYLEM.)

The phloem of gymnosperms and ferns is made of irregularly shaped cells with many sieve plates on all surfaces. (*See* FERN; GYMNOSPERM.) These plants have no companion cells.　　A.J.C./M.J.C.; M.H.S.

PHLOX (fläks) *Phlox* is a genus of flowering plants that includes about sixty-five species, all but one of which are native to North America. Phlox belong to the family Polemoniaceae.

Most phlox are perennials. (*See* PERENNIAL PLANT.) Their simple leaves occur in opposite pairs close to the ground but often become alternate higher up. (*See* LEAF.) Their brilliant flowers grow in clusters, each flower having five petals.

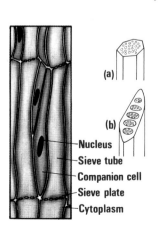

Phloem tissue in angiosperms (left) contains two kinds of living cells—sieve tubes and companion cells. Companion cells have nuclei, which control the working of the sieve tubes. Fluids pass from one sieve tube to another through sieve plates. The two kinds of sieve plates are (a) simple and (b) compound.

Nucleus
Sieve tube
Companion cell
Sieve plate
Cytoplasm
(a)
(b)

Blue phlox is noted for its gorgeous flowers that bloom in the spring.

Summer phlox (*Phlox paniculata*) grows to heights of 60 in. [150 cm]. It is a popular garden plant in eastern North America. Blue phlox (*Phlox divaricata*) is noted for its blue or white flowers that bloom each spring.

J.M.C./M.H.S.

PHOEBE (fē′bē′) The phoebe is a small bird that belongs to the flycatcher family, Tyrannidae. It has a large head, slender bill, and long tail, which it twitches frequently. There are three species of phoebe in North America: the black phoebe in the southwest, Say's phoebe in the west, and the eastern phoebe in the east. Phoebes eat insects and nest in rock crevices, under bridges, and beneath overhanging porches. *See also* BIRD.　　S.R.G./L.L.S.

PHOSPHATE (fäs′fāt′) Phosphates are compounds that contain phosphorus, oxygen, and at least one other element. They always include the ion PO_4^{-3}. (*See* COMPOUND; IONS AND IONIZATION.) Phosphates are found in many different minerals. The most important phosphate is calcium phosphate. Calcium phosphate is found in bones and is used as a fertilizer. If calcium phosphate is treated with sulfuric acid, calcium hydrogen phosphate is formed. Calcium hydrogen phosphate is used in fertilizers called superphosphates. It dissolves in water and can be more easily absorbed by plants than calcium phosphate. This makes it a better fertilizer. *See also* FERTILIZER; MINERAL.　　M.E./A.D.; E.D.W.

PHOSPHORESCENCE (fäs′fər res′ənts) Phosphorescence is a way that certain materials give off light by means other than heat. (*See* INCANDESCENCE; LIGHT.) An atom is made up of electrons moving around a central core called a nucleus. (*See* ATOM.) The electrons move around in orbits. Each orbit is a different distance from the nucleus. Electrons in a higher (farther) orbit have more energy than electrons in a lower (nearer) orbit. When radiation is applied to certain materials, their electrons absorb the energy and move into a higher orbit. (*See* RADIATION.) The electrons are said to be excited. At some point, the electrons give out the energy as light and drop back to their original orbit. If light is given off by the electrons long after the radiation is

Phosphates are used as fertilizers on farms throughout the world.

removed, it is called phosphorescence. (*See* FLUORESCENCE.)

Substances that are naturally phosphorescent include eggshells and ivory. Phosphorescent minerals include barium sulfide, calcium sulfide, and strontium sulfide. Some organisms, such as fireflies, glowworms, jellyfish, and certain tiny sea animals, are phosphorescent. This characteristic is called bioluminescence. *See also* BIOLUMINESCENCE; LUMINESCENCE.   C.C; M.E./S.S.B.; L.W.

PHOSPHORIC ACID (fäs fȯr'ik as'əd) Phosphoric acid (H_3PO_4) is a compound that contains hydrogen, phosphorus, and oxygen. (*See* COMPOUND.) It is an essential component of DNA and RNA in body cells. (*See* DNA; RNA.) Phosphoric acid is used in soft drinks, food additives, and fertilizers.

M.E./A.D.; E.D.W.

PHOSPHORUS (fäs'fə rəs) Phosphorus (P) is a solid nonmetallic element. (*See* ELEMENT.) Phosphorus occurs in several different forms. These different forms are called allotropes. (*See* ALLOTROPE.) The best-known form is called white or yellow phosphorus because of its color. White phosphorus is a poisonous, waxy solid with a relative density of 1.8. (*See* RELATIVE DENSITY.) It is very reactive and may catch fire in air. Therefore, it is stored under water. If white phosphorus is heated to 480°F. [250°C] or is exposed to sunlight, it changes into another allotrope called red phosphorus. Red phosphorus is not as reactive as white phosphorus and does not catch fire in air. Red phosphorus is not poisonous and is slightly heavier than white phosphorus. Its relative density is 2.2.

Phosphorus was discovered in 1669 by Hennig Brand, a German alchemist. (*See* CHEM-ISTRY, HISTORY OF.) It is used in making matches and smoke bombs. The most important compounds of phosphorus are salts called phosphates. Phosphates are salts of acids called phosphoric acids. (*See* PHOSPHATE; PHOSPHORIC ACID.) Phosphorus is essential to life. Bones are mainly made of calcium phosphate.

The atomic number of phosphorus is 15, and its atomic weight is 30.9738. It melts at 111.4°F. [44.1°C] and boils at 536°F. [280°C].   M.E./J.R.W.

PHOTOELECTRIC EFFECT The photoelectric (fōt'ō i lek'trik) effect is any effect in which light energy is converted to electricity. Examples of photoelectric effect usually fall into one of three categories—photoemission, photoconductivity, or photovoltaics. The device that makes use of the photoelectric effect is often called a photoelectric cell, a photo cell, or an electric eye.

A device that makes use of the photoelectric effect is the photoelectric trigger on the remote flash unit of a camera (above). When the flash unit goes off, the light is sensed by the photoelectric trigger. The trigger then sets off the flash unit again. The trigger allows a sequence of flashes to take place without having to connect the flash units with cables.

Photoemission was first explained by Albert Einstein. (*See* EINSTEIN, ALBERT.) Light, like all other radiation, is made up of small particles called photons. (*See* PHOTON.) The amount of energy the photons have depends on the frequency of the light. The frequency of light is the number of times that a light wave vibrates in a second. (*See* FREQUENCY.) The higher the frequency, the more energy the photons have. If a photon hits an atom of a certain material (called a photoemittive material), it may be absorbed by an electron of that material. (*See* ATOM; ELECTRON.) However, if the photon has enough energy, the electron is ejected, or emitted, from the atom. In this way, light energy changes into electrical energy. (*See* ELECTRICITY.) If wires are attached to a photoemittive material, the electrons can flow along the wires, forming an electric current.

Photoemission cells are used in motion picture projectors to read film sound tracks. The sound track is printed in a pattern on the edge of the film. A beam of light passes through the sound track and activates a photoemission cell in the projector. The varying width of the sound track produces a varying amount of light that is converted into electrical impulses. These electrical impulses are then converted into sound impulses.

Photoconductivity results from light hitting a semiconductor. (*See* SEMICONDUCTOR.) Semiconductors contain free, negatively charged electrons. A free electron is an electron that has left its atom and so is not bound to it. When the electron leaves its atom, it creates a positive charge in the atom. The positive charge attracts an electron from another atom. This process repeats itself, creating an electric current. When light falls on certain semiconductors, the number of electrons leaving their atoms increases. This increases the current. A streetlight is a good example of an application of photoconductivity. As daylight fades, the electrical current in the streetlight's semiconductor comes to a stop. This activates a switch that turns the streetlight on.

Burglar alarms sometimes have electric eyes that operate on the principle of photoconductivity. When the light source to the semiconductor is interrupted by a person walking through the beam of light, a switch is activated that triggers the alarm. Other examples of electric eyes include automatic door openers and elevator doors. In an automatic door opener, a light shines on a photoelectric cell, producing an electric current. The electric current keeps the doors closed. If the light source is blocked by a person wanting to go through the door, the photoelectric cell stops producing a current, and the door opens. A similar reaction occurs when a person blocks the light of an electric eye in elevator doors. This causes the doors to either stay open until every passenger has passed through or to reopen if they have started to close.

The photovoltaic effect is similar to photoconductivity. In this effect, light falls on two semiconductors, or on a metal and a semiconductor sandwiched together. A boundary develops between these two substances. Free electrons build up along the boundary but cannot flow across it. However, if the two substances are connected in a circuit, then the electrons can flow across the boundary and through the circuit. Photovoltaic cells are used in exposure meters for photography. (*See* EXPOSURE METER.) Light falling on the meter causes a current to flow. The size of the current depends on the amount of light. The light can be measured indirectly by measuring the current. Solar cells work on the same principle. *See also* SOLAR CELL.   C.C./L.W.

PHOTOGRAPHY (fə tăg′rə fē) Photography is the process of taking pictures with a camera. (*See* CAMERA.) The word *photography* means "drawing with light." A photograph is a picture "drawn" with rays of light.

Photography enriches our lives in many ways. Illustrations in newspapers, magazines, and books are usually photographs. Photography is an important tool in advertising, business, and industry. It helps people explore the earth, the oceans, and outer space. Some photographs have lasting artistic value.

Photography is one of the most popular hobbies in the world. For example, almost half the families in the United States own a camera. Many people all over the world join camera clubs to meet with other camera enthusiasts. Sometimes, they display their photographs at exhibitions in art galleries and museums.

Motion picture making and video recording are branches of photography. Many principles used in regular photography are used in making motion pictures and videotapes. (*See* MOTION PICTURE; VIDEO RECORDING.)

Today's cameras have many features that make taking pictures easier than it was in the past. For example, many cameras now have built-in exposure meters and lenses that focus automatically. (*See* EXPOSURE METER; LENS.) Some cameras also have electronic chips that recognize difficult picture-taking situations, such as when a person is standing in front of a brightly lit window. (*See* CHIP.) The chip directs adjustments to be made by various computer parts, so that the photograph is properly exposed.

Exposing the film Proper lighting is the key to taking good photographs. Too much light reaching the film results in photographs that are overexposed. Such photographs have little detail and look foggy. If color film is used, many of the colors do not show up, and the image appears very light. On the other hand, too little light reaching the film results in photographs that are underexposed. Such

Camera "safaris" are popular with wildlife photographers. They provide the opportunity to take photographs of many different kinds of animals, such as the turtle below, in their natural surroundings.

This photograph is overexposed.

This photograph is underexposed.

This photograph is correctly exposed.

photographs are too dark. Many details do not show up because of the overall darkness.

Films are made with different speeds, or sensitivities to light. Some films are very sensitive. They are called "fast" films. A fast film is able to take photographs in situations in which there is little light. A fast film is also used when a high shutter speed is needed, such as when photographs are being taken of a fast-moving object. The shutter is the device that allows light to enter the camera. A disadvantage of a fast film is that the photographs can be "grainy" looking. Other films are called "slow" films. Slow films are less sensitive to light than fast films. Slow films can only be used in situations in which there is adequate light. However, slow films produce photographs that are very sharp and show fine detail. In the United States, film speed is set by the American Standards Association (ASA). Slow films generally are numbered under 80. Medium-speed films are numbered from 80 to 125. Fast films are generally numbered over 125.

The exposure of film can be varied in two major ways. First, the exposure time, during which the shutter of the camera is open, can be altered. Second, for any given exposure time, the amount of light entering the camera can be increased or decreased. This is done by changing the size of the aperture, or lens opening, with a diaphragm that blocks off part of the lens. Several different combinations of aperture settings and shutter speeds make it possible to get the proper settings for all conditions of light. The selection depends on the particular type of photographer's subject being photographed, the effect required, and the camera involved.

A device called an exposure meter, or light meter, can be used to measure the brightness of the scene being photographed. (*See* EXPOSURE METER.) This enables a suitable aperture to be chosen. Most exposure meters work on a photoelectric principle. (*See* PHOTOELECTRIC EFFECT.) Many cameras have built-in meters. In dim lighting conditions, such as the interior of a building, an exposure of several seconds may be necessary. Most cameras have a setting that allows the shutter to be held open as long as necessary. Electronic flash units may be used to illuminate the scene or subject in dim light conditions. The flash is synchronized with the opening of the shutter. Flash units, which are built into the camera or attached to it, can also be used in complete darkness.

Developing and printing in black and white

Black-and-white film has a light-sensitive coating of tiny grains of silver bromide. When these grains are exposed to light, they tend to break down and deposit dark grains of silver. However, this process is only completed through the chemical actions of a solution of developer. During development, parts of the film that were most exposed to light deposit the most silver and become dark. Meanwhile, unexposed places remain unchanged. In a later stage, called fixing, the unchanged grains are dissolved away, leaving clear film. After fixing, the film is washed and dried. All gradations between dark and bright occur according to the pattern of light in the scene photographed. However, what was light in the scene becomes dark in the developed film, and vice versa. Thus, the developed film is called the negative.

Printing is the process of reversing the dark and light tones of the negative into light and dark tones on the paper. The picture obtained is called a positive. The simplest form of printing is contact printing, in which the negative is in contact with the paper. The printing paper is coated with a light-sensitive emulsion, just as the film is. After a brief exposure to a bright light, it is developed, fixed, washed, and dried much like film.

Most photographic printing is done by enlarging and not by contact printing. This is because actual-size prints from most film would be too small for general use. In enlarging, a bright, magnified image of the negative is projected onto the printing paper. Development is then finished as described above.

Color photography

Color photography is more complicated than black-and-white. Light that looks white to our eyes is really a mixture of all colors of the rainbow. (*See* LIGHT.) Any color can be reproduced by blending only three basic colors such as blue, green, and red. These colors are called primary colors of light. In color photography, blue light, red light, and green light are blended in certain proportions to produce any color. (*See* COLOR.)

There are two types of color film: (1) negative and (2) reversal. Negative film produces color negatives from which color prints are made. Reversal film produces color transparencies (slides). A slide is usually viewed in a lighted slide viewer or through a projector that shines the colored picture onto a screen.

Negative and reversal films are made in almost the same way. Each consists of three layers of emulsion on a sheet of plastic. These emulsions are similar to the emulsions on black-and-white film, but each emulsion is sensitive to only one of three primary colors. The first emulsion is affected only by blue light, the second only by green light, and the third only by red light.

Many photographers enjoy developing and printing their own pictures.

When color film is exposed, light passes through the first emulsion and records an image of the blue areas of the scene. A special yellow filter layer prevents unused blue light from reaching the other two primary color layers. Then the light passes through the second emulsion layer, which records only the green areas of the scene. Finally, the light passes through the third emulsion layer, which records the red areas.

Color negative film is developed in a special developer. A silver image forms in each emulsion layer. The developing solution then causes colored dyes to form in each layer by reacting with substances called couplers. A yellow dye forms in the first layer. A magenta (bluish red) dye forms in the second layer, and a cyan (bluish green) dye forms in the third layer. These three colors are complementary, or direct opposites, to the three primary colors of light—blue, green, and red. Complementary colors reproduce the original colors when light is passed through the film.

Each dye acts as a filter to a primary color. The yellow dye absorbs blue light and lets red and green light pass through. The magenta dye absorbs green light and lets red and blue pass through. The cyan dye absorbs red light and lets blue and green pass through. In this way, the original colors of the subject appear in a print.

Color reversal film that produces color slides has a similar developing process. However, there is one extra step. The film is re-exposed after the first development. During the second development, colored dyes form around the silver images of the subject. The silver is then bleached out, leaving transparent film in those areas. In the developed film, a yellow dye surrounds the image made by blue light, magenta dye surrounds the green light image, and cyan dye surrounds the red light image. When the film is projected, each dye holds back light of the complementary color, and the original colors of the subject appear on the screen. (*See* POLAROID CAMERA.)

Photography and electronics   Since the 1980s, electronics has played a large role in photography. (*See* ELECTRONICS.) For example, a kind of specialty camera called an electronic still camera is now available. Electronic still cameras work in much the same way as adjustable cameras. However, instead of recording the image on film, electronic still cameras store the image in digital form on a special kind of floppy disk. (*See* COMPUTER.) Storing the image digitally means that different segments of the image are given a number code. The photographer can do several things with such an image. For example, the floppy disk can be inserted into a device called a disk drive that is similar to the disk drives used with computers. The disk drive is attached to a home television set and is used to display the image on the television. The image can be reproduced using the disk drive and a printer similar to those used with computers. The image may also be sent quickly to another location by a device called a modem, which is often built into the camera. A modem is an electronic device that allows information to be sent or received, usually over telephone lines. Communicating by modem has many advantages for photographers. For example, a newspaper photographer can take a photograph in one city. He or she can then connect the modem in the camera to a telephone and send the picture to his or her newspaper many miles away.(*See* MODEM.) The receiving computer can store the image on another disk, display it, or print it.

Another electronic advancement in photography is called electronic image manipulation. This process allows a photographer to change his or her photograph after it has been taken. First, the photograph is passed through a device called an optical scanner. The scanner converts the image into digital signals that can be understood by a computer. The photographer views the image on a display screen that resembles a television screen. The photographer uses a hand-held device called a "mouse," to manipulate the image he or she sees. For example, suppose a photograph had a blue flower in its background. Electronic image manipulation allows the photographer to change the color of the flower and place it in a different position in the photograph. Parts of a photograph may also be removed and replaced with parts from another photograph. After the photographer is finished making changes, the new photograph can be printed out on paper. The print can then be fed into a special device that reproduces the image on film.

P.Q.F.; W.R.P./R.W.L.; L.W.

PHOTOMETRY (fō tăm′ə trē) Photometry is a branch of science concerned with the measurement of light. Instruments that measure the brightness of artificial light sources are called photometers. Photometers most often use a standard light source. The light source that is to be measured is compared to the standard source. The photometer is placed between these two sources. Some of the light from each source passes through prisms. (*See* PRISM.) The prisms deflect the light into an eyepiece. The distance from the photometer to the light sources is then adjusted. At a certain distance, the two sources look equally bright in the eyepiece. By using the inverse square law, scientists can calculate the brightness of the unknown source. (*See* INVERSE SQUARE LAW.)

A different method is used for measuring the brightness of daylight. A device called a barrier layer cell is used. This is made of a metal and a piece of selenium. Selenium is a nonmetallic element. When light falls on the cell, a voltage develops in it. (*See* PHOTO-ELECTRIC EFFECT.) This causes a current to flow in a circuit that contains an ammeter or voltmeter. The size of the current depends on the brightness of the daylight. In this way, the brightness of the light can be measured. This system is used in exposure meters for cameras. *See also* CANDELA; EXPOSURE METER; FLUX; FOOT-CANDLE; LIGHT; LUMEN.   M.E./S.S.B.

PHOTON (fō′tän′) In many ways, light behaves like a wave. For example, light exhibits interference and diffraction. (*See* DIFFRAC-TION; INTERFERENCE; WAVE.) These are wave effects. However, the wave theory of light cannot explain certain phenomena related to light. These can only be explained by regarding light as a stream of particles. These particles are called photons. They were first proved to exist by Albert Einstein in 1905. (*See* EINSTEIN, ALBERT.)

Light is a form of electromagnetic radiation. All electromagnetic radiation, such as radio waves and ultraviolet rays, consists of photons. *See also* ELECTROMAGNETIC RADIATION; LIGHT; PHOTOELECTRIC EFFECT.

M.E./R.W.L.

PHOTOPERIODISM (fōt′ō pir′ē əd iz′əm) Photoperiodism is the response of a living organism to the length of day or night, or both. The photoperiod, also called the critical day length, is the number of hours of light needed to cause this response. Some examples of photoperiodism are the migration of some birds and the breeding of many animals. (*See* BIOLOGICAL RHYTHM; MIGRATION.)

Photoperiodism most commonly refers to the appearance of flowers on a flowering plant. Short-day plants, such as poinsettias and strawberries, flower when the day is shorter than a certain number of hours. Most short-day plants bloom in the early spring or late

Photoperiodism is the response of a living organism to the length of day or night, or both. Some plants, such as the lettuce above, are long-day plants. This means they bloom when daylight lasts longer than a certain number of hours. Most long-day plants bloom in the summer.

fall. Long-day plants, such as spinach and lettuce, flower when the day is longer than a certain number of hours. Most long-day plants bloom in the summer. Neutral-day plants are not affected by the length of the day.

Photoperiodism in plants is controlled by a light-sensitive, bluish pigment called phytochrome. (*See* PIGMENT.) Florists often use their knowledge of photoperiodism to produce flowers year-round. They do this by artificially controlling the lengths of the "days" and "nights" in greenhouses where the flowers are grown.

A.J.C./M.H.S.

PHOTOSYNTHESIS (fōt′ō sin′thə səs) Photosynthesis is the process by which green plants and certain other organisms make food. It is a complex series of chemical reactions that uses energy from sunlight to make food and oxygen from carbon dioxide and water—all in the presence of the pigment chlorophyll. (*See* CHLOROPHYLL.)

Without chlorophyll, photosynthesis cannot take place. In higher plants, chlorophyll is found in structures called chloroplasts. Most of the chloroplasts are found in the cells of the plant's leaves. (*See* LEAF.) Water is absorbed by the roots and taken to the leaves. (*See* ROOT.) Air containing carbon dioxide enters the leaves through tiny openings called stomata (plural of *stoma*). (*See* STOMA.) These substances that the plant takes in are essential for photosynthesis.

The food made by photosynthesis is glucose, a simple sugar. (*See* GLUCOSE.) Glucose is distributed throughout the plant and used by the cells and tissues as a source of chemical energy. Some of the glucose is combined with nitrogen to form amino acids, proteins, or nucleic acids. (*See* AMINO ACID; NUCLEIC ACID; PROTEIN.) Nitrogen is usually dissolved in

All green plants, such as the organ-pipe cactus at left, carry out a chemical process called photosynthesis. During this process, the plants use energy from sunlight to make food and oxygen from carbon dioxide and water.

water absorbed by the roots. Some of the glucose is changed to cellulose and used to build up plant tissues. (*See* CELLULOSE.) Some of the glucose is also changed to starch and stored in the leaves, stem, or roots.

Food for almost all living organisms comes either directly or indirectly from photosynthesis. Many animals eat plants for food. Other animals—including human beings—eat plants and plant-eating animals. Thus, photosynthetic plants are a vital part of the food chain. (*See* FOOD CHAIN.)

Most plants and animals get the energy they need through respiration. (*See* RESPIRATION.) In respiration, food and oxygen are used to make energy, carbon dioxide, and water. Thus, respiration and photosynthesis are opposite reactions and occur in a continuous cycle. The end products of one reaction are the raw materials needed for the other.

Photosynthetic organisms probably produced most of the oxygen in the atmosphere as the earth was developing. Since that time, the amount of oxygen in the air (about 21 percent) and the amount of carbon dioxide in the air (about 0.04 percent) have remained fairly constant as a result of photosynthesis. (*See* AIR.)

Of all the photosynthesis that takes place, more than 75 percent takes place in the oceans, in tiny organisms called phytoplankton. (*See* PLANKTON.) Scientists are constantly seeking ways to use these marine organisms as a food source for human beings. Scientists are also trying to find ways of increasing the amount of photosynthesis that takes place in land plants in hopes of increasing the world

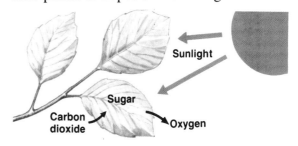

In photosynthesis, carbon dioxide from the air is used to make sugar, and oxygen is released into the air.

food supply. They have found that factors such as temperature, light intensity, water supply, and carbon dioxide supply all affect the rate of photosynthesis. The rate, however, is limited by factors such as enzymes that affect rates of many of the chemical reactions in photosynthesis. *See also* ATP; CARBON CYCLE; WATER CYCLE.   A.J.C./M.H.S.

PHOTOVOLTAICS *See* PHOTOELECTRIC EFFECT.

PHYLUM (fi′ləm) A phylum, in the classification of living organisms, is a subdivision of a kingdom. It is made up of a group of related classes. In the four kingdoms other than the plant kingdom, the term *division* is often used instead of *phylum*. *See also* CLASS; CLASSIFICATION OF LIVING ORGANISMS; KINGDOM.

A.J.C./M.J.C.; C.R.N.

PHYSICAL CHANGE A physical (fiz′i kəl) change is any change that happens to a substance without affecting its chemical composition. For example, a physical change occurs when ice melts to form water. Both ice and water have the same chemical composition: H_2O. Therefore, there is no chemical change. The change is a physical change. If the ice had broken down into hydrogen and oxygen, then this would be a chemical change.

In many solids, the atoms are arranged in a regular pattern. This pattern is called a crystal lattice. (*See* LATTICE.) The lattice always has a definite shape. Under very high pressures, the shape of the lattice can be altered. This is another example of a physical change. Many properties of solids depend on their lattice shape. Changing the lattice shape can sometimes change the physical properties of a solid. For example, very high pressures can

change a solid that conducts electricity into one that does not.

M.E./A.D.

PHYSICS (fiz′iks) Physics is the study of the properties of matter and energy. Physicists try to understand these properties in the universe. They do this by observing and performing experiments. They use their observations and the results of their experiments to derive laws. The laws can be used to predict the results of other experiments. Laws are descriptions of natural phenomena. However, they do not explain why such phenomena occur.

Physicists propose theories to explain why certain events take place. For example, Sir Isaac Newton's theory of mechanics explains how and why things move the way they do. (*See* NEWTON, SIR ISAAC.) Theories change as physicists make new observations and do new experiments. For example, Newton's theory of mechanics was accepted for more than two hundred years, until the beginning of this century. However, experiments on objects moving at almost the speed of light could not be explained by Newton's theory. A new theory, the theory of relativity, was devised by Albert Einstein to explain these new results. (*See* EINSTEIN, ALBERT; RELATIVITY.)

Most physical laws are stated mathematically. Mathematics is a very important and powerful tool for physicists. For example, many experiments in physics involve measurements. Physicists also use mathematics to develop, expand, and apply new theories in physics.

Physics is divided into a number of different branches, including mechanics, heat, light, sound, electricity and magnetism, and solid-state physics. There are also branches that cover atomic, nuclear, and particle physics.

Mechanics is the study of solid bodies and fluids and the forces that act on them. The action of forces on solid bodies is studied in two main branches: statics and dynamics. Statics is the study of forces acting on a body at rest, such as the forces acting on a bridge. Dynamics is the study of forces that cause bodies to move, such as the forces acting on a swinging pendulum. (*See* MECHANICS.)

Heat studies are concerned with the effect of temperature on various substances. Heat is a form of energy. It can be changed into different forms of energy such as mechanical or electrical energy. Thermodynamics is the study of such transformation of energy. (*See* HEAT; THERMODYNAMICS.)

The study of light is called optics. It includes investigations of the nature and properties of light. An important part of optics is the study of optical instruments such as telescopes and microscopes. (*See* OPTICS.)

Sound is studied in a branch of physics called acoustics. Acoustics is the study of properties of sound, such as the ways in which sound is transmitted through air and other materials and how sound, is produced. (*See* ACOUSTICS.)

Electricity and magnetism were once considered to be two separate subjects. During the 1800s, however, several connections were discovered between them. Electricity and magnetism are now studied as a single subject. The study of the connections between electricity and magnetism is called electromagnetism. (*See* ELECTRICITY; ELECTROMAGNETISM; MAGNETISM.)

Solid-state physics is a recently developed branch of physics. It explains the properties of a solid in terms of its atoms. One of the results of solid-state physics has been the invention of the transistor. Transistors largely replaced

vacuum tubes in many electronic devices. Another result of solid-state physics has been the invention of the integrated circuit. An integrated circuit combines the work of several transistors. (*See* INTEGRATED CIRCUIT; SOLID-STATE PHYSICS; TRANSISTOR; VACUUM TUBE.)

Atomic, nuclear, and particle physics are also newer branches of physics. Atomic and nuclear physics include the study of the atom and the nucleus. Particle physics is the study of subatomic particles. (*See* PARTICLE PHYSICS.) The mathematics needed for these subjects is very advanced. Many of the properties of atoms, nuclei, and particles are explained by quantum theory. *See also* QUANTUM THEORY.

M.E./J.T.; E.D.W.

PHYSICS, HISTORY OF Physics (fiz′iks) is the study of the properties of matter and energy in the universe. Physics started with the ancient Greeks. They studied it together with biology, chemistry, and astronomy under the title "natural philosophy." (*See* PHYSICS.)

One of the greatest Greek thinkers was Aristotle. Aristotle developed theories on motion and many other subjects in physics. Many of his ideas were accepted until the 1500s. (*See* ARISTOTLE.) Archimedes, another Greek scientist, did experiments with levers and floating bodies. Some of his laws are still used today. (*See* ARCHIMEDES.)

After the Greeks, little scientific progress was made in Europe until the 1500s. However, the Arabs translated and preserved many of the Greek writings. They also made their own contributions to science.

During the 1500s, the Polish astronomer Nicolaus Copernicus gathered evidence that the earth traveled around the sun. This went against the established opinion, which followed Aristotle's view—that the sun traveled around the earth. A few years later, Johannes Kepler showed that the orbits of the planets were not quite circular. The orbits were ellipses (ovals). This also went against established opinion. In time, Copernicus's and Kepler's view came to be accepted by the scientific community. (*See* COPERNICUS; KEPLER, JOHANNES.)

Experiments in physics were not really performed until 1600. In that year, the English scientist Sir William Gilbert wrote the first scientific study of magnetism. (*See* GILBERT, WILLIAM.) Gilbert suggested his ideas about magnetism and demonstrated them with experiments. Another great practical physicist of the 1600s was the Italian physicist Galileo Galilei. (*See* GALILEO.) Galileo showed that two different weights fall at the same speed if neither is too light. A light weight is noticeably slowed down by air resistance. According to popular legend, he is supposed to have demonstrated this by dropping weights from the Leaning Tower of Pisa. In addition to discovering laws about the motion of bodies, Galileo also improved the recently invented telescope (*See* TELESCOPE.) He used the telescope to show that the earth moves around the sun. His opponents refused to look through his telescope. They stopped him from writing and from continuing his experiments.

One of the most important scientists of the 1600s was Sir Isaac Newton. (*See* NEWTON, SIR ISAAC.) Newton's theory of gravity explained the orbits of the planets. In mechanics, his laws of motion were accepted for more than two hundred years. In optics, Newton was the first to show that white light is a mixture of light of different colors. He demonstrated that light consisted of small particles,

which he called corpuscles. At the same time, a Dutch physicist, Christian Huygens, did experiments that light was made up of waves. The modern understanding of light combines both Newton's and Huygen's ideas.

During the 1700s, scientists started to investigate heat and electricity. At first, scientists thought that heat was a fluid, because when it "flowed" into a material, the material became hot. The experiments by Count Rumford and James Joule showed that heat was a form of energy instead. (*See* JOULES, JAMES PRESCOTT.)

In the early 1800s, the theory that matter is made up of tiny particles that came to be called atoms became well-known. The chemist John Dalton found that atoms combined to form molecules. (*See* ATOM; DALTON, JOHN; MOLECULE.)

Scientists realized that the movement of atoms or molecules caused an object to feel hot. This led to the kinetic theory of gases. This theory helped explain a number of earlier laws about gases. These discoveries about heat led to the development of thermodynamics. Thermodynamics is the study of ways in which heat energy can be turned into other forms of energy. Thermodynamics helped explain how a steam engine works.

Electricity and magnetism were known to the ancient Greeks. They tried unsuccessfully to explain these forces. Electricity began to be studied again in the 1700s. The American scientist Benjamin Franklin studied different kinds of electricity—including lightning. (*See* FRANKLIN, BENJAMIN.) During the 1800s, great steps were made in understanding electricity. The most important work was done by an English physicist, Michael Faraday. (*See* FARADAY, MICHAEL.) He discovered that a wire with a current flowing in it acts as a magnet. His discoveries are the basis of the modern method of generating electricity. (*See* ELECTROMAGNETISM.) In 1873, a Scottish physicist, James Clerk Maxwell, produced a series of equations to describe electricity and magnetism. His equations used the idea of an electromagnetic field. (*See* FIELD; MAXWELL, JAMES CLERK.) Using his equations, Maxwell was able to describe a wave. This wave moved through the electromagnetic field. He found that these waves were exactly the same kind as light waves. Maxwell had managed to combine optics with electricity and magnetism. In 1886, a German physicist, Heinrich Hertz, discovered another kind of electromagnetic wave, the radio wave. (*See* HERTZ, HEINRICH.)

By the end of the 1800s, physicists thought that all the important laws of physics had been discovered. Then a number of discoveries were made that could not be explained. The French physicists Antoine Becquerel and Marie and Pierre Curie discovered that the atoms of some substances were unstable. They gave off particles and radiation called gamma rays. These substances are said to be radioactive. (*See* BECQUEREL, ANTOINE HENRI; CURIE FAMILY; RADIOACTIVITY.) Uranium and radium, for example, are radioactive. Radioactivity could not be explained until later scientists developed new theories about the structure of the atom.

Another discovery that could not be explained was how certain substances produce an electric current when exposed to light. This is called the photoelectric effect. Only certain frequencies of light generate a current in a particular substance. In 1900, German scientist Max Planck proposed a theory that helped explain the photoelectric effect. Planck proposed that light is given off in packets or particles called quanta (plural of *quantum*). Each quantum has a specific amount of energy, depending on the light's frequency. This theory, called the quantum theory, helped explain how light produces an electric current in particular substances. (*See* FREQUENCY: PHOTOELECTRIC EFFECT; PLANCK, MAX; QUANTUM THEORY.)

In 1913, a Danish physicist, Niels Bohr, produced a model of the atom. During the

Along with being an important statesman, Benjamin Franklin was an accomplished scientist. Among other things, he studied the different forms of electricity, including lightning.

1920s, two German physicists, Werner Heisenberg and Erwin Schrödinger, improved Bohr's model. (*See* BOHR, NIELS; HEISENBERG, WERNER; SCHRÖDINGER, ERWIN.) With their theory, many effects were explained for the first time. In 1911, the English physicist Ernest Rutherford discovered that an atom has a central core called a nucleus. (*See* NUCLEUS, ATOMIC; RUTHERFORD, ERNEST.) During the 1920s and 1930s, the nucleus came to be well understood, and radioactivity was explained. It was discovered that the nucleus itself is made of even smaller particles. These particles are called protons and neutrons. Since that time, scientists studying the atom have learned that protons and neutrons are made up of even smaller particles. These particles are called elementary particles. Many elementary particles have been discovered in recent years. (*See* PARTICLE PHYSICS.)

Another important theory of this century is the theory of relativity. (*See* RELATIVITY.) It was discovered by the German-American physicist Albert Einstein. (*See* EINSTEIN, ALBERT.) Relativity largely replaced Newton's theory of mechanics. It also gave scientists a more in-depth understanding of gravity.

These modern theories have led to many new discoveries and inventions. The nucleus of the atom contains a great deal of energy. Once the nucleus was understood, its energy could be tapped. The energy of the nucleus is now used to provide electricity in nuclear power plants. It is also used to build nuclear weapons.

The study of elementary particles has enabled great advances to be made in electronics. For example, radio and radar used to be based on vacuum tubes. Now they use integrated circuits. One tiny chip of silicon may contain thousands of electronic components. Such developments could only have happened with a knowledge of elementary particles and quantum theory. (*See* ELECTRONICS.)

Astrophysics, too, is a relatively new branch of physics. It applies the theories and methods of physics to determine the structure of heavenly bodies and to solve other problems in the ancient science of astronomy. *See also* ASTROPHYSICS.   M.E./A.I.; E.W.L.

PHYSIOLOGY (fiz′ē äl′ə jē) Physiology is the study of the functioning of living things. Plant physiologists study how plants work. Animal physiologists study the functioning of various animals' organs and systems. Human physiologists examine the actions of structures and organs in the human body. They learn how these structures and organs work when healthy and when diseased.

Physiology, anatomy, and biochemistry are closely related. (*See* ANATOMY; BIOCHEMISTRY.) Anatomy includes the study of the shape and parts of an organism. Biochemistry is the study of the chemicals that make up an organism and the chemical changes that go on in living things. For example, the anatomist studies the structure of the stomach muscles and glands. The biochemist studies the chemicals that make up the stomach cells and the chemical changes that occur when the cells pour gastric juices into the stomach. Physiologists are interested in discovering what body activities make the cells secrete gastric juices when food enters the stomach. They also study the churning movements of the stomach.

Physiology is also closely related to medicine and to pathology, the study of disease. (*See* MEDICINE; PATHOLOGY.) In most diseases, parts of the body are not acting the way they should. Doctors study physiology to understand how the healthy body functions. This knowledge allows them to better understand how diseases affect people.

One example of the benefits of physiological research has been control of the disease diabetes mellitus. Diabetes mellitus develops when certain parts of the pancreas do not act the way they should. (*See* DIABETES.) Less than one hundred years ago, many people used to die of this disease each year. In 1922, physiologists Frederick Banting and Charles Best completed a long series of experiments with animals. (*See* BANTING, SIR FREDERICK GRANT.) These experiments helped them develop a treatment for diabetes mellitus in humans. This treatment has since saved the lives of thousands of diabetic people.

W.R.P./M.C.; J.J.F.; M.H.M.

PHYSIOTHERAPY (fiz′ē ō ther′ə pē) Physiotherapy, also known as physical therapy, is the use of any physical means and/or exercise to treat a disease or injury. It is part of the branch of medicine called rehabilitation medicine. Doctors who specialize in this branch of medicine are called physiatrists. Treatments prescribed by these doctors are given by specially trained people called physical therapists.

Physiotherapy is helpful in treating many kinds of disabilities and diseases. It is often used in treating various kinds of paralysis and muscle weaknesses that occur from stroke, poliomyelitis, or multiple sclerosis. (*See* MULTIPLE SCLEROSIS; POLIOMYELITIS; STROKE.) It is also used in treating heart and lung diseases. Physiotherapy can be prescribed as treatment for amputations, fractures, and other injuries. With the aid of physiotherapy, the disabled person gains the capability to lead a more constructive and creative life.

Many kinds of devices and treatments are used in physiotherapy. Radiant heat lamps, electric heating pads, diathermy (electric heat treatment), hydrotherapy (water treatment), and special baths are used to apply heat to diseased or damaged parts of the body. Heat relieves pain and improves circulation. Cold, used immediately after certain injuries, lessens pain and swelling. Ultraviolet radiation is used to attack pathogens (disease-causing organisms) and to help healing. Ultrasound is used to treat inflammatory conditions of muscles and joints. (*See* INFLAMMATION; ULTRASOUND; ULTRAVIOLET RAY.)

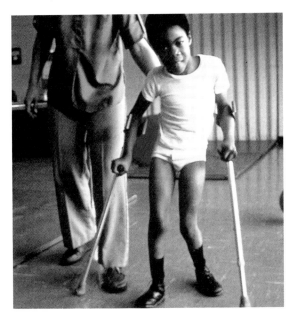

Physiotherapy involves the use of exercise and/or physical devices to treat disease and injury. The child above is receiving physiotherapy to learn how to walk with crutches.

Exercise is an important part of physiotherapy. Physical therapists help patients exercise, and they encourage patients to do many physical things on their own. Often, they work with equipment such as pulleys, weights, parallel bars, and stationary bicycles. Splints, braces, crutches, and wheelchairs also help disabled patients perform daily activities.

Physical therapists help people learn to use all of these devices and develop confidence in doing daily tasks.

Physical therapists work in clinics, hospitals, and schools for the handicapped. To practice in the United States, they must be licensed. *See also* MEDICINE.

W.R.P./J.J.F.; M.H.M.

PIAGET, JEAN (1896-1980) Jean Piaget was a Swiss psychologist who is best known for his work in the field of child psychology. He suggested the theory that a child's mental abilities, like his or her physical abilities, develop (grow) in a certain order through a series of specific steps.

The four stages of development, as suggested by Piaget, are sensory-motor, pre-operational, concrete operations, and formal operations. In the sensory-motor stage (birth to two years old), a child learns about objects, or things, through the use of his or her senses—tasting, smelling, hearing, seeing, and touching objects. In the preoperational stage (two to seven years old), a child begins calling objects by their names. This is the beginning of language for the child. In the concrete operations stage (seven to eleven years old), a child begins to think logically. The child understands likenesses and differences, such as those used in naming objects. The child has begun to think in an organized way. In the formal operations stage (eleven years old to adulthood), the child begins to think abstractly. The child can understand abstract words and concepts such as space, time, and freedom.

From the time Piaget was a young child, he was interested in science. He published a scientific paper when he was only ten years old. He received a doctor's degree in science in 1918. Piaget used his interest in science for his work in psychology. He was among the first to take a biological approach to understanding the development of mental abilities. His theories are widely accepted and respected throughout the world. *See also* PSYCHOLOGY.

A.J.C./D.G.F.

PICCARD, AUGUSTE (1884-1962) Auguste Piccard was a Swiss scientist who was born in Basel. He had a twin brother, Jean Felix, who was also a scientist. In 1932, Auguste Piccard used a balloon to fly up to the stratosphere (the second layer of the atmosphere). In order to go this high, Piccard invented a pressurized cabin—that is, a cabin in which air pressure was kept at a normal level in spite of the altitude. He showed that flying at high altitudes was possible. Piccard reached an al-

Auguste Piccard

titude of 52,657 ft. [16,050 m]. (*See* ATMOSPHERE.)

In 1945, Piccard made a a spherical steel cabin called a bathyscaphe to help him go down to great depths in the ocean. The bathyscaphe protected him from the water pressure at these depths. Piccard's bathyscaphe reached a depth of 35,800 ft. [11,000 m]. *See also* BATHYSPHERE AND BATHYSCAPHE.   C.M./D.G.F.

PICKEREL (pik′ə rəl) A pickerel is a freshwater fish that belongs to the pike family, Esocidae, and is closely related to the northern pike. (*See* PIKE.) The three species of pickerels are the bulldog pickerel, the mud pickerel, and the chain pickerel. All these fishes have long, slender bodies; long, pointed snouts; and many sharp teeth. They are greenish in color.

Pickerels live in shallow, weedy lakes or slow-moving rivers. They stay very still near a log or rock, waiting for a small animal to swim by. When one swims near, the pickerels dart out very quickly and take the prey in their teeth. Pickerels eat small fish, frogs, snakes, and insects.

Bulldog and mud pickerels rarely grow beyond 12 in. [30 cm] in length, so they are not often sought by fishers. The chain pickerel, however, grows to lengths over 24 in. [60 cm]. It is a popular game fish.   S.R.G./E.C.M.

PIEZOELECTRIC EFFECT If certain crystals are pressed or stretched, an electric voltage develops across the crystal. This is called the piezoelectric (pē ā′zō′i lek′trik) effect. If a voltage is applied to a piezoelectric crystal, the crystal expands or contracts. This is called the reverse piezoelectric effect. (*See* CRYSTAL; CURRENT, ELECTRIC; VOLT.)

Piezoelectric crystals have many uses. The expansion or contraction of a crystal can be used to produce sound waves. Therefore, piezoelectric crystals are used to convert electrical signals into sound waves and vice versa. For example, they are used in telephone mouthpieces to convert sound into an electrical signal. In the earpiece of a telephone, the electrical signal is converted back into sound

by another piezoelectric crystal. Such crystals are also used in microphones and in the pickup cartridge (which holds the needle) of record players.

Another important use for piezoelectric crystals is in sonar equipment. Sonar equipment is used on ships and submarines. Sonar makes sound waves under the water. The waves are used to find underwater objects. The waves are produced by the vibrations of a piezoelectric crystal. If an object is present, the waves are reflected off the object. A piezoelectric crystal then picks up the reflected wave and turns it into an electrical signal. In this way, objects under the water are displayed on a screen. (*See* SONAR.)

An alternating voltage is a voltage that varies. The voltage decreases in one direction to zero. Then it builds up in the opposite direction. It again decreases to zero and then increases in the original direction. If an alternating voltage is applied to a piezoelectric crystal, the crystal vibrates. It expands when the voltage goes in one direction. Then the crystal returns to its normal size as the voltage decreases to zero. The crystal contracts when the voltage goes in the opposite direction. The atoms in a crystal have a natural frequency of vibration. Frequency means the number of vibrations that occur per second. (*See* FREQUENCY.) If the frequency of the voltage is the same as the natural frequency of the crystal, then the crystal resonates. (*See* RESONANCE.) This means that it vibrates very strongly. This effect is used in radio broadcasting. Quartz crystals are used for broadcasting because they resonate at the required frequency. Quartz crystals are also widely used in other piezoelectric devices because they are very stable, even at high temperatures. *See also* QUARTZ.

M.E./L.L.R.

Early breeds of pigs domesticated from wild boars tended to have most of their weight in the front part of their bodies (top). Pigs on today's farms have been bred so that most of their weight is concentrated in their hindquarters, or hams (bottom).

PIG Farmyard pigs, or hogs (also called swine), are descended from the wild boars that roamed throughout Asia, Europe, and north Africa thousands of years ago. Many scientists believe that people began taming pigs about 8,500 years ago. It is believed that such pigs were used as village scavengers, that is, to clean up rubbish. Pigs were useful as scavengers because they are omnivorous— they eat almost anything. (*See* OMNIVORE.)

The European wild boar (*Sus scrufa*) is the animal from which many of today's domestic hogs are descended. In the early 1800s, Spanish and French explorers brought domestic hogs to North and South America. Until the 1940s, United States farmers classified hog breeds as one of two kinds—lard type or meat type. Lard-type hogs had more fat in proportion to lean meat. Meat-packing plants made the fat into lard. This lard was used for cooking and other purposes. In the 1950s, shortening made from vegetable oils began to replace lard. Since then, farmers have raised hogs mainly for their meat.

Many different breeds of pigs have been developed in various parts of the world to meet local climate and pasture conditions. (*See* BREEDING.) Farmers in the United States raise about twenty breeds of hogs, including Landrace, Tamworth, and Yorkshire pigs.

A sow (adult female pig) gives birth to eight to twenty piglets (baby pigs) at a time, two or three times a year. Pigs reproduce rapidly and can be mated when about eight months old. Sows carry their young about 114 days before they farrow (give birth). A piglet weighs only about 2.5 lb. [1.1 kg] at birth but gains weight quickly, usually doubling its weight the first week. When it is only one year old, a piglet can weigh 250 lb. [113 kg]. The average boar (adult male pig) weighs from 350 to 500 lb. [159 to 230 kg]. The average sow weighs from 300 to 450 lb. [140 to 404 kg]. Most pigs are marketed when they are about six or eight months old, weighing from 180 to 240 lb. [82 to 109 kg]. Pigs kept beyond this age are usually used for breeding purposes.

An adult female pig gives birth to eight or more piglets at a time.

The pig's snout has a flat, tough disk on the end that includes the nostrils. Hogs have canine teeth that develop into sharp tusks. These tusks serve as tools for digging and as weapons for fighting. They are much larger on males than on females.

Pork, ham, bacon, and spareribs all come from the meat of pigs. A pig's meat can be smoked or salted and then kept for a long time without spoiling. Pig intestines are used as the casing for sausages. Besides its use as food, the pig has other uses. The pig's hide, when tanned, becomes the leather known as pigskin. Pigskin is used to make such items as gloves and luggage. The stiff bristles from the pig's hide are made into paintbrushes and hairbrushes. Pig's blood is used in animal feed, fertilizer, and medicine. J.J.A./J.J.M.

The iron that is made in blast furnaces, above, is called pig iron. Today, most pig iron is used to make steel.

PIG IRON Pig iron is the name for all iron made in blast furnaces. (*See* BLAST FURNACE; IRON.) It is not pure iron, but usually contains about 95 percent iron, 3 or 4 percent carbon, and smaller amounts of other elements, such as sulfur, phosphorus, and manganese.

In a pig-casting machine, the molten (liquid) iron flows into molds. The term *pig* comes from an early method of running hot iron into sand molds arranged around a main channel like a litter of pigs around the mother.

Today, most pig iron is used to make steel. The molten iron is carried from the blast furnaces to "mixers," which are huge heated tanks. Mixers keep the iron in liquid form until it is used by the steel-making furnaces. *See also* STEEL.

J.J.A./A.D.

PIGMENT (pig′mənt) In chemistry, pigment is a substance, often in the form of a powder, that gives color to another material. Pigment colors a material in one of two ways—it is mixed in with the material or applied over its surface in a thin layer.

Pigments, such as the ones at left being sold in a market in Peru, are often in the form of a powder. Pigments do not dissolve when mixed with a liquid; they stay suspended in it.

Pigment does not dissolve but rather remains suspended in a liquid. For example, when pigment is suspended in a certain kind of liquid, it forms paint. (*See* PAINT.) Colored substances that dissolve in liquids (giving color by staining) are called dyes. (*See* DYE.)

Pigments also occur in nature. In biology, a pigment is any substance that colors the tissues or cells of organisms. *See also* ALBINO; COLOR; PIGMENTATION; SKIN. J.J.A./E.R.L.

PIGMENTATION (pig′mən tā′shən) The coloring of a living organism is nearly always caused by the presence of one or more coloring substances called pigments. (*See* PIGMENT.) In plants and animals, the pigments are in the cells of the organisms' outer layers.

The main pigment in human coloration is melanin. This dark-colored pigment is found in the skin and hair. The color of skin is determined by the amount of this pigment. People who are native to sunny regions tend to have large amounts of melanin and are dark brown or nearly black. The high melanin content has evolved in these races because it protects the underlying layers of skin from sunburn. People who are native to cooler and less sunny regions tend to have paler skins. With the exception of albinos, however, all people have some melanin in their skin. (*See* ALBINO.) People with light-colored skin can produce more melanin when their skin is exposed to extra sunlight. Their skin turns browner. This process is known as tanning.

Melanin is also responsible for hair color. Dark hair contains much melanin. Blond hair has only a little. Red-haired people, who often have pale skin, also have little melanin.

Many animals, such as chameleons, cephalopods, and flatfish, can change their appearance by altering the distribution of pigments in their skin. Nerves or hormones cause the pigment granules (small grains) to scatter or become smaller, thereby changing the color of the skin. *See also* CAMOUFLAGE; HORMONE.

J.J.A./C.R.N.

PIKA (pē′kə) The pika is a small, furry mammal related to the hare and rabbit. (*See* MAMMAL.) Pikas are found in Asia, Europe, and North America. The animals often live among loose rock on mountainsides. Some kinds of pikas live together in large groups called colonies.

The pika is a small, furry animal often found in the loose rocks on mountainsides. Pikas spend much of their time collecting and storing plant material that they will eat during the winter months.

The American pika (*Ochotona princeps*) is frequently called a conie or a calling hare. American pikas are about 7 in. [18 cm] long, not including the tail. Their coat is grayish brown on the back with white or light brown covering the underside. American pikas resemble guinea pigs. Collared pikas (*Ochotona collaris*) are also found in North America. Like the American pika, the collared pika lives in the mountains. The collared pika, however, lives farther north than the American pika.

Pikas feed on plants. The animals spend much time collecting grasses and other plants to use during the winter months. Pikas store these foods by stacking them in piles that look like small haystacks. *See also* HARE; RABBIT.

J.J.A./J.J.M.

PIKE (pīk) Pikes are freshwater fishes belonging to the pike family, Esocidae. Members of this family include the pickerels and the muskellunge. (*See* MUSKELLUNGE; PICKEREL.) Perhaps the best-known member is the northern pike. The northern pike is found in northern lakes and rivers of Europe, Asia, and North America. It hides near a rock or a log, sitting very still. When a small animal, such as a frog, insect, or small fish, swims by, the pike darts out and grabs the prey in its sharp teeth.

The northern pike is one of the most popular game fishes in North America. It has been widely stocked into waters in which it did not previously live. The largest pike caught by a North American fisher was over 46 lb. [20 kg]. Like its relatives, the muskellunge and pickerels, the northern pike is a very strong fighter.

S.R.G./E.C.M.

PILING (pī′ling) Piling is a method of making a strong foundation for a building, bridge, or other large structure. Piling is used when the upper layers of soil are too weak to support an ordinary foundation. Piling is also used to retain water and soil—for example, to protect a beach from erosion. (*See* EROSION.)

Piles are long pieces of timber, concrete, or steel. They are usually driven into the ground, though concrete piles may be cast in position. A pile driver may use a weight to batter a pile into position. A vibrating pile driver shakes a pile into the ground. *See also* BRIDGE; BUILDING CONSTRUCTION; SOIL MECHANICS.   J.M.C./R.W.L.

Piles are columns of timber, concrete, or steel that are usually driven into the ground to support structures such as the dock at left.

PILOT FISH The pilot (pī′lət) fish is a salt-water fish that belongs to the family Carangidae. It is white or pale blue with dark vertical bands on its sides. It is called a pilot fish because it is usually seen swimming near large fish and whales. It was once believed that the

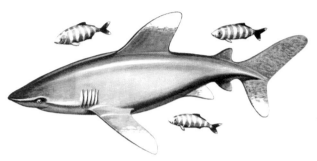

Pilot fish usually swim near large fish, such as this shark, and whales.

pilot fish guided the large animals to food. Ichthyologists—scientists who study fish—now believe that pilot fish swim near large fish because it is easier for them to swim in the currents caused by the large fish. The pilot fish grows to a length of about 24 in. [60 cm]. It is found in the Pacific and Atlantic oceans.

S.R.G./E.C.M.

PILTDOWN MAN Piltdown (pilt′daŭn′) man was the name given to the fossil remains of a supposed prehistoric human being. The fossils were discovered in 1912 in a gravel pit at Piltdown, England. In 1955, the fossils were proven to be fake.

The fossils consisted of a skull and jawbone. The braincase seemed very modern, while the jaw was quite apelike. Analyses completed in the 1950s proved that the skull was of a human being who had lived about 750 years before. The jaw was that of a modern ape. The jaw had been stained by chemicals to make it appear older, and the teeth had been artificially ground down to make them appear human.

For forty years, Piltdown man caused an amazing scientific uproar. The hoax did, however, have the positive effect of stimulating the development of new methods of finding the age of fossils. *See also* DATING; FOSSIL; HUMAN BEING. J.M.C./S.O.

PINEAL GLAND The pineal (pī′nē əl) gland is an endocrine gland found in vertebrates (animals with backbones) near the center of the brain. (*See* ENDOCRINE.) The role of this pea-sized gland is unclear. The pineal gland is thought to secrete (give off) the hormone melatonin. (*See* HORMONE.) Melatonin has been found to affect the growth of the sex glands in some young animals. In certain adult animals, it seems to regulate the activity of the sex glands. In human beings, melatonin may determine when a person reaches sexual maturity. It may also help regulate the menstrual cycle in women. (*See* MENSTRUAL CYCLE.)

Some scientists have suggested that the pineal is a vestigial sense organ. (*See* VESTIGIAL ORGAN.) The exact function of the pineal gland remains uncertain. *See also* HORMONE.

J.M.C./J.J.F.

PINEAPPLE (pī′nap′əl) The pineapple (*Ananas comosus*) is a fruit-bearing plant belonging to the bromeliad family, Bromeliaceae. The plant probably originated in Brazil. It is grown today in tropical areas throughout the world.

The pineapple plant grows to heights of 2 to 3 ft. [60 to 90 cm]. Its leaves are sword-shaped and spiny. Purplish flowers grow in clusters on thick stalks. (*See* INFLORESCENCE.) Each of these flowers produces a small, fleshy fruitlet. These fruitlets fuse together to form one large fruit, the pineapple. The fruit weighs from 4 to 6 lb. [2 to 4 kg]. Its firm flesh is a

The pineapple is one of the most popular tropical fruits. It originated in Brazil, but today it is grown in tropical regions throughout the world.

light yellow color. The group of leaves at the top of the fruit is called the crown. Although most pineapples have small brown seeds, a popular variety, called smooth cayenne, is seedless.

Pineapple plants require a warm climate and a moderate amount of water. Chemicals are often spread over the area where pineapples are planted to prevent damage to the plants by parasitic worms. (*See* PARASITE.) Plastic strips are sometimes laid down between the plants to help the soil retain nutrients and water.

Nearly one-third of the pineapples produced each year are cultivated in Hawaii. Other important pineapple-producing areas are in Brazil, Malaysia, and Mexico. *See also* FRUIT.

J.M.C./M.H.S.

PINE FAMILY The pine (pīn) family includes more than 250 species of coniferous trees. (*See* CONIFER.) Members of this family have needlelike leaves that grow in small clusters or in spirals around the stem. The male and the female reproductive structures are in different cones on the same plant. (*See* MONOECIOUS.) Pine trees, which belong to the genus *Pinus*, are among the most common trees in this family. Other members of the pine family include cedar, Douglas fir, fir, hemlock, larch, and spruce.

There are about one hundred species of pine trees. They are found throughout the world, mostly in the northern hemisphere. Huge forests of pine trees grow across Canada and the northern United States.

There are two types of pine trees: soft, or white, pines; and hard, or yellow, pines. The soft pines include the largest and the oldest pines. The sugar pines of California and Oregon sometimes grow to a height of 248 ft. [75 m]. The bristlecone pines are among the

There are approximately one hundred species of pine trees. Lodgepole pines are shown at left below. The cones of a pine tree are shown at right below.

oldest living trees. Some are almost five thousand years old and are still alive.

The hard pines include some of the most valuable lumber trees in North America. Pine trees provide lumber that is important in the construction, furniture, and paper industries. (*See* LUMBER; PAPER.) Pines are also sources of oil, turpentine, charcoal, and fuel gases (by-products produced by distillation). *See also* EVERGREEN; GYMNOSPERM.   A.J.C./M.H.S.

PINK FAMILY The pink family includes more than two thousand species of herbaceous plants. They are dicotyledons and grow throughout the world. (*See* DICOTYLEDON; HERBACEOUS PLANT.) The leaves grow in opposite pairs and have smooth margins. (*See* LEAF.) The stem is swollen at the nodes, where the leaves attach. The flowers usually grow in clusters.

Genus *Gypsophila* includes fifty species of plants known as baby's breath. These plants produce tiny pink or white flowers, which are often added to bouquets of other flowers as trim. The most popular members of the pink family belong to genus *Dianthus*. This genus includes the carnations, sweet williams, and pinks.   A.J.C./M.H.S.

PIPEFISH (pīp'fish') A pipefish is a snake-like saltwater fish that belongs to the family Syngnathidae. It is related to the sea horse. (*See* SEA HORSE.) The pipefish has a long, thin body. Pipefish range in length from 1 to 20 in. [2.5 to 50 cm]. There are twenty-one species of pipefish in North America. They live in both the Atlantic and Pacific Oceans. Pipefish eat plankton. *See also* PLANKTON.   S.R.G./E.C.M.

PIPETTE (pī pet') A pipette is a piece of glass apparatus used in chemistry and biology. It is used for transferring an exact volume of a liquid from one container to another.

A pipette consists of a cylindrical glass bulb. At each end of the bulb there is a length of thin glass tubing. The lower end of the pipette has a thin tip. A rubber bulb is placed on the upper end of the pipette. The end without the rubber bulb is placed in the liquid to be transferred. The rubber bulb is squeezed and then released to draw the liquid up the pipette. The upper part of the tube has lines marked on it. The pipette is filled to the appropriate line. The pipette now holds an exact volume of the liquid. This can be transferred to another container.   M.E./R.W.L.; E.D.W.

PIRANHA (pə rän'yə) A piranha is a sharp-toothed freshwater fish that belongs to the family Characidae. It is native to lakes and rivers throughout most of South America. Piranhas eat large amounts of prey and may attack land animals that fall into the water. Despite their reputation, they rarely attack people. Piranhas grow to be 24 in. [60 cm] long. They are often kept in the United States as aquarium pets, though it is illegal to do so in some states because of the danger of their being released into water bodies. They have been introduced into some North American rivers and lakes both by aquarium owners who tired of them and as game fish.

S.R.G./E.C.M.

PISTIL (pis'təl) The pistil is the female reproductive structure of a flower. It usually has three parts: stigma, style, and ovary. The stigma is at the top of the pistil. It has a sticky surface that will hold any pollen grains that land on it. (*See* POLLINATION.) The stigma leads to the tubelike style, which opens into the ovary. In some plants, the style is missing, and the stigma is directly on top of the ovary. Ovules are produced in the ovary. The ovules contain the female gametes, or eggs. (*See* OVARY; OVULE.)

The number of pistils in a flower varies by species. Some flowers have many pistils; some have none. Some flowers have a compound pistil—actually several pistils fused into one. *See also* FLOWER; FRUIT; REPRODUCTION.   A.J.C./M.H.S.

PITCH (pich) Pitch is a black, gluelike substance that is left behind when petroleum or coal tar is distilled. (*See* DISTILLATION.) It is called asphalt in its natural form. (*See* ASPHALT.) Pitch is water repellent and highly adhesive. (*See* ADHESION.) It is used for roof coatings, highway paving, and waterproofing applications.   W.R.P./J.M.

PITCHBLENDE (pich′blend′) Pitchblende is an important ore of the radioactive metal uranium. It occurs in igneous rocks, mainly granite, and in veins of iron, copper, lead, and tin minerals. Pitchblende is usually brown, black, or dark gray. It consists mainly of the com-

A miner drills a tunnel in a pitchblende mine.

pound uranium oxide. It also contains small amounts of other elements, such as radium, thorium, and zirconium. Pitchblende is a type of uraninite. See *also* COMPOUND; ELEMENT; MINERAL; ORE; ROCK; URANINITE; URANIUM.

M.E./R.H.

PITOT TUBE A pitot (pē tō′) tube is used for measuring the rate at which a gas or a liquid flows. For example, a pitot tube can be placed inside a pipeline to measure the rate at which a gas or a liquid flows through the pipeline. A pitot tube can also be fitted onto an airplane to measure the speed of the air flowing past the airplane. This lets the pilot determine how fast he or she is moving relative to the rate of flow of the air. This is called the air speed of the airplane.

The pitot tube was invented by a French engineer, Henri Pitot, during the 1700s. A pitot tube is a narrow metal tube that is bent at a right angle. One end has a nozzle that faces into the fluid flow. Since the tube is small, it hardly disturbs the flow. In pipelines, the other end of the pitot tube is connected to a manometer. A manometer is an instrument that measures differences in pressure. (*See* MANOMETER.) The reading on this manometer is due to two different sorts of pressure in the pitot. One is called the dynamic pressure. This is caused by the gas or liquid moving through the pitot. There is also static pressure. This is the pressure exerted by the fluid even when it is not flowing. To calculate the rate of flow, only the dynamic pressure is needed. Therefore, the static pressure must be subtracted from the reading on the manometer. The static pressure is measured by another manometer. Then the rate of flow can be calculated.   M.E./R.W.L.

PITUITARY GLAND *See* HORMONE.

The rattlesnake at left is a pit viper. Notice the pit, or shallow hole, between the snake's eye and nostril. These pits (there is one on each side of the head) have heat-sensitive areas that help the pit viper locate its warm-blooded prey, such as mice and rabbits.

PIT VIPER Pit vipers are poisonous snakes that belong to the viper (vī′pər) family. (*See* VIPER.) The pit vipers are distinguished from the true vipers by the two pits—or shallow holes—that are found between their eyes and nostrils. These pits are sensitive to heat. They help the snakes locate warm-blooded prey such as small mammals. (*See* MAMMAL.) Rattlesnakes, copperheads, and cottonmouths are the pit vipers native to North America. The only other poisonous snake in North America is the coral snake. *See also* SNAKE.   S.R.G./R.L.L.

PLACENTA (plə sent′ə) The placenta is an organ that is formed during pregnancy to allow substances to be exchanged between the blood of the mother and the fetus (the unborn young). Among all the members of the animal kingdom, only mammals have a placenta. The only mammals that do not develop a placenta are the pouched marsupials and the egg-laying monotremes. (*See* MAMMAL; MARSUPIAL; MONOTREME.)

In the placenta, the blood of the fetus comes very close to, but never mixes with, the blood of the mother. Digested food, water, oxygen, hormones, and antibodies move by diffusion from the mother's blood into the fetus's blood. Waste products diffuse from the fetus's blood into the mother's blood. In a sense, then, the mother eats, breathes, and removes wastes for her unborn child. (*See* ANTIBODY; DIFFUSION; HORMONE.)

The placenta forms from tissues surrounding the fetus and from some of the tissues in the

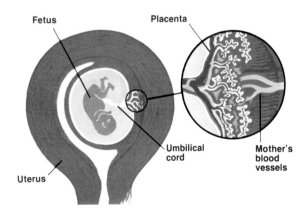

In its mother's uterus, the fetus, in effect, feeds, breathes, and excretes wastes through the placenta. The placenta is connected to the fetus by the umbilical cord.

mother's uterus. The placenta develops small, fingerlike villi, which are bathed directly in the mother's blood. Blood flows through the umbilical cord to and from the villi. (*See* UMBILICAL CORD.) The umbilical cord connects the fetus to the placenta. In human beings, the placenta is almost fully formed within the first two months of pregnancy. Throughout the pregnancy, the placenta also makes hormones that are needed for the pregnancy to continue and progress in a healthy manner.

Soon after the baby is born, the placenta is given off along with other membranes, all of which is called the afterbirth. However, some mammals do not force out the placenta, but instead take it back into their system. *See also* PREGNANCY.

A.J.C./M.J.C.; J.J.F.; M.H.M.

PLANCK, MAX (1858-1947) Max Planck was a German physicist famous for developing the quantum theory. He was born at Kiel and studied in Berlin.

Max Planck

In 1900, while he was a professor in Berlin, Planck developed the theory that energy behaves as if it is given off as particles. He called

these particles of energy quanta (plural of *quantum*). At first, Planck's idea was not taken seriously.

Gradually, scientists realized that the quantum theory helped explain things they could not explain any other way. In 1918, Planck was awarded the Nobel Prize for physics for his work. Today, both wave and quantum theories are used to describe different aspects of energy in physics. *See also* LIGHT; PHOTON; QUANTUM THEORY; WAVE.

C.M./D.G.F.

PLANCK'S CONSTANT *See* QUANTUM THEORY.

PLANE FAMILY The plane (plān) family consists of one genus (*Platanus*) with ten species of large, deciduous trees that are native to temperate areas of North America, Europe, and Asia. (*See* DECIDUOUS TREE.) The members of this family have large, palmately lobed (resembling a hand with fingers spread) leaves.

Trees in the plane family are native to temperate areas of North America, Europe, and Asia. The American sycamore (above) is the largest member of the plane family.

(*See* LEAF.) Each plant has both male flowers and female flowers. (*See* MONOECIOUS.) Although separate, they are closely grouped in thick round heads. The fruit is a knobby ball that has many seeds.

The American sycamore (*Platanus occidentalis*) is the largest member of the plane family. It sometimes reaches a height of more than 165 ft. [50 m]. *See also* SYCAMORE.

A.J.C./M.H.S.

PLANET (plan'ət) A planet is a body that revolves around a star. A planet gives off no light of its own. It can be seen because it reflects light from the star. It also receives most of its heat from the star. (*See* ASTRONOMY; STAR.)

The solar system   There are nine major planets in orbit around the star called the sun, helping make up the solar system. (*See* SOLAR SYSTEM; SUN.) A major planet is different from a minor planet, such as an asteroid, because of its size and the shape of its orbit. (*See* ASTEROID; ORBIT.) In the order of the increasing average size of their orbits, the major planets are Mercury, Venus, Earth, Mars, Jupiter, Saturn, Uranus, Neptune, and Pluto. Except for Mercury and Pluto, they all orbit in approximately the same plane (level). The rest of this article will focus on these major planets.

A planet may be orbited by one or more smaller, solid bodies called satellites, or moons. Seven of the nine planets of the solar system are known to have moons. (*See* MOON; SATELLITE.)

Astronomers think that other stars in the universe may be orbited by one or more planets. In 1983, they found evidence that a star called Vega has a shell of solid particles surrounding it. These particles probably formed from the materials that formed the star. Many astronomers believe the solid particles may eventually form a solar system around Vega. However, the tremendous distance from Earth of this and other stars makes the search for other planets very difficult.

When viewed from Earth, other planets seem to give off a steady light, while stars twinkle. Because planets are relatively near Earth, their motion against the background of stars is noticeable. Because the stars are so distant, they appear to remain in the same position. Actually, the stars are moving thousands of times faster than any of the planets.

The planets are divided into two main groups: the terrestrial planets and the Jovian planets. The terrestrial planets—Mercury, Venus, Earth, and Mars—are similar in size and have solid, rocky surfaces. *Terrestrial* means "relating to land." (*See* EARTH; MARS; MERCURY; VENUS.) The Jovian planets are Jupiter, Saturn, Uranus, and Neptune. The name *Jovian* means "relating to Jupiter." The planets are called Jovian because Saturn, Uranus, and Neptune—like Jupiter—consist largely of

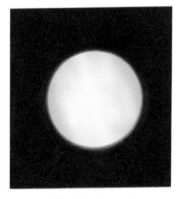

Neptune, one of the Jovian planets, consists largely of gases.

gases. The Jovian planets are also very large. Scientists put the farthest planet, Pluto, in a category by itself. Scientists know little about the surface of Pluto because it is so far away. However, they believe Pluto is made up of frozen gases. This makes Pluto's surface more similar to those of the terrestrial planets than those of the Jovian planets. (*See* JUPITER; NEPTUNE; PLUTO; SATURN; URANUS.)

Pluto and Neptune are too far from Earth to be seen without a telescope. The other planets can be seen in the night sky. Mercury, because of its closeness to the sun, is visible only briefly after sunset or before sunrise.

Planet movements Each planet follows an elliptical (oval) orbit around the sun. As a planet orbits, it turns, or rotates, on its axis (an imaginary line running through its center). The closer a planet is to the sun, the less time it takes for it to complete its orbit. Mercury completes its orbit in 88 days. Pluto, the most distant planet, takes about 248 years. (For about 20 years every 248 years, Pluto's orbit is inside Neptune's. Most recently, this period began in 1976. Pluto will again be the most distant planet in 1999.) All the planets orbit in a counterclockwise direction.

The closer a planet is to the sun, the faster its orbital speed. Mercury, the closest, has a velocity (speed in one direction) of 30 mi. [48 km] per second. Pluto, the farthest, travels at 2.7 mi. [4.7 km] per second. Earth's velocity is about 18 mi. [30 km] per second. That translates to about 66,240 m.p.h. [106,580 kph].

Of the terrestrial planets, Earth rotates on its axis once every 24 hours. Mercury takes 59 days, Venus takes 243 days, and Mars takes 24 hours and 37 minutes. Pluto takes 6 days, 9 hours, and 18 minutes. The other Jovian planets show less variation, ranging from about 10 to 18 hours. Venus and Uranus rotate clockwise. The other seven planets rotate counterclockwise.

All the planets except Mercury have a tilted axis. No two planets rotate on the same tilt. Earth's axis is tilted about 24° to the orbital plane. Uranus is tilted about 98° to the orbital plane.

Properties of the planets The characteristics of the planets are due in part to their distance from the sun. The planets closer to the sun have higher temperatures than the more distant planets. A planet's atmosphere also affects how much of the sun's light and heat are absorbed.

Earth is unlike the other planets in many ways. It is apparently the only planet that can sustain life as we know it. Earth is the only planet with an atmosphere that is rich in oxygen.

Of all the planets, Mercury orbits closest to the sun. Its orbit averages about 36 million mi. [57.9 million km] from the sun. Until recently, Mercury was believed to have no atmosphere. However, experiments have shown that Mercury probably has a very thin atmosphere that comes from the solar wind. (*See* SOLAR WIND.) The temperature on Mercury's surface reaches about 800°F. [427°C] during the day. At night, the temperature falls to about 70°F. [21°C]. Photographs of Mercury's surface taken by space probes show it to be crater-marked rock. Space probes are unmanned spacecraft that are equipped with very advanced sensing, recording, and transmitting instruments. (*See* SPACE TRAVEL.) In composition, Mercury seems to be more like our moon than like any of the other planets. There is no evidence that Mercury ever had a thicker atmosphere or any bodies of water.

Venus was once thought to be much like Earth. Space probes, however, have found it to be very different. The planet is surrounded by dense clouds of sulfuric acid. (*See* SULFURIC ACID.) Beneath the clouds, lightning

Venus is often the brightest object in the night sky other than the moon.

flashes constantly, but no rain falls. The planet has the least elliptical orbit, but it rotates clockwise. This means that, on Venus, the sun appears to rise in the west. The clouds around Venus are in three layers. A clear atmosphere of carbon dioxide extends from the planet's surface to the dense bottom cloud layer. This distance is about 19.9 mi. [32 km]. The other clouds of the atmosphere contain several gases, including nitrogen and water vapor. The planet's temperature is higher than the boiling point of sulfur, about 900°F. [470°C]. The temperature is much cooler at the planet's poles, however. There is no measurable magnetic field and no seasonal change.

Venus's orbit is the closest to Earth. It is often the brightest object in the night sky other than the moon. Venus is often called the Evening Star or Morning Star because it is usually visible in the three hours after sunset or the three hours before sunrise.

Earth's other neighboring planet is Mars. Mars is barely more than half of Earth's diameter. A coating of dust stained by iron oxide gives the planet a reddish appearance when viewed through a telescope. Most of its surface is covered by sand dunes and rocks. Temperatures vary from near 70°F. [21°C] at noon to about -150°F. [-100°C] at night. Mars is the only other planet besides Earth that has water on its surface. However, the water on Mars is mostly in the form of ice caps at the poles. Mars has a very thin atmosphere, which includes a trace of water vapor. Astronomers think the cap at the south pole may be mostly frozen carbon dioxide (dry ice). Mars's surface is dotted with huge volcanoes that were active when the planet was young. Space probes and satellites have revealed traces of erosion that seems to have been caused by flowing water, but no sign of life has been found.

Mars has a reddish appearance due to a coating of dust stained by iron oxide (above). Its surface is sandy and rocky (below).

Jupiter, Saturn, Uranus, and Neptune are all much larger than any of the other planets. However, they are also much less dense than the other planets. They are mostly balls of helium and hydrogen. They all spin much more rapidly on their axes (plural of *axis*) than do the smaller planets. Jupiter spins the fastest of all the planets. All sides of each planet can be observed by telescope during a single night. All four planets are orbited by one or more rings. Jupiter's thin ring consists mainly of dust particles. Saturn has seven rings, made up of particles and blocks of frozen gas, dust, and ice. Saturn's rings are much brighter than Jupiter's or Uranus's. Uranus has at least eleven semitransparent rings made up of chunks of unknown black material.

Neptune is a stormy planet. Above the planet, clouds of methane are pushed by winds of up to 1,500 m.p.h. [2,414 kph]. There is a permanent storm system in Neptune's southern hemisphere that is as large as Earth. Scientists call this system "The Great Dark Spot." Scientists have recently learned that Neptune has four complete and several incomplete rings circling it.

Like the other Jovian planets, Pluto is very cold compared with Earth. In fact, Pluto is the coldest of all the planets. Astronomers think its surface temperature is near -459.67°F. [-273.15°C], which is absolute zero. (*See* ABSOLUTE ZERO.)

The planets differ greatly in density and mass. (*See* DENSITY; MASS.) The density of Saturn is less than that of water. Pluto may have about the same density as water. The density of the other Jovian and the terrestrial planets is more than that of water. The largest of the Jovian planets, Jupiter, has 318 times the mass of Earth. The smallest planet, Pluto, has about 0.0017 times the mass of Earth. The planets also differ in gravity. (*See* GRAVITY.) Gravity does not affect the density or mass of an object. However, it does affect the weight of an object. An object weighs more if the force of gravity is stronger. For example, a person who weighs 120 lb. on Earth would weigh 46 lb. on Mercury or Mars, 109 lb. on Venus, and 304 lb. on Jupiter.

This picture shows Saturn (with rings) and six of its moons.

This is an artist's idea of how the Viking 1 space probe looked as it landed on Mars in 1976.

Space probes have helped scientists learn more about the planets than they could have ever learned from Earth. The *Mariner* and the *Viking* space probes that traveled through space in the 1960s and 1970s helped scientists learn about Mercury, Venus, and Mars. *Pioneer X* and *Pioneer-Saturn* were launched in the 1970s to study Jupiter and Saturn. All of those probes were launched by the United States. The *Venera* space probes, which were launched by the Soviet Union in the 1960s, 1970s, and 1980s, studied Venus. In 1983, the *Pioneer X* space probe passed out of Earth's solar system. However, it is still transmitting information. *Voyager 1* and *Voyager 2* were launched by the United States in 1977. *Voyager 1* sent back photographs of Jupiter and Saturn, but its equipment started failing as it passed Saturn. *Voyager 2* proved to be one of the most successful space probes ever launched. *Voyager 2* sent back photographs of Jupiter, Saturn, Uranus, and Neptune. In the early 1990s, *Voyager 2* is expected to pass out of Earth's solar system. However, *Voyager 2* will continue to send information back to Earth. *Magellan* was launched by the United

Jupiter (upper right) is shown with four of its moons.

States in 1989. In 1990, it started sending back information about Venus.

Scientists have also used orbiting space telescopes that send images back to Earth. The space telescopes are observatories designed to orbit around Earth, as opposed to space probes, which travel through the solar system and beyond. Between 1969 and 1988, the United States placed over seventy space telescopes in orbit around Earth. These telescopes studied the sun as well as the planets. Some of the telescopes that studied Earth sent back information about the movements of Earth's crust and the movements of weather patterns in Earth's atmosphere. The first large reflecting space telescope, the Hubble Space

Telescope (HST), was launched into orbit in 1990. However, one of the mirrors of the HST was manufactured incorrectly. Because of this, some of the first images sent back to Earth were distorted. *See also* OBSERVATORY; TELESCOPE.   C.C.; P.Q.F.; G.Z./G.D.B.; D.H.M.; L.W.

PLANETARIUM (plan′ə ter′ē əm) A planetarium is a model or device that shows the positions and movements of certain heavenly bodies. The oldest type of planetarium is called an orrery. An orrery is a mechanical device that represents the sun as a large ball, the planets as slightly smaller balls, and moons as still smaller balls. These balls can be moved to portray the movements of the heavenly bodies. (*See* MOON; PLANET.)

Many museums and universities have planetariums where projectors are used to cast an image of the night sky on a domed ceiling. In this way, the sky in different parts of the world or the skies during the different seasons can be shown. The projectionist, often an astronomer, may give a lecture describing the projection and discuss a wide range of astronomical phenomena.

The Adler Planetarium in Chicago was one of the first planetariums constructed in the United States to use a projector that displays the moon, planets, stars, and sun on an overhead dome. The Adler Planetarium shows each object moving as it does in the natural sky. Since the Adler Planetarium was built, other cities have also constructed planetariums to teach astronomy. *See also* ASTRONOMY.

J.M.C./E.W.L.; C.R.

A planetarium is a model or device that shows the position and movements of certain heavenly bodies. Pictured above is the planetarium at the University of Arizona at Tucson.

PLANKTON (plangk′tən) Plankton includes all small, floating organisms that live in bodies of water. Algae and tiny floating plants are called phytoplankton. Phytoplankton accounts for most of the world's photosynthesis and releases large amounts of oxygen into the air. (*See* PHOTOSYNTHESIS.) Protozoans and tiny floating animals are called zooplankton. Fish eggs and larvae are also considered zooplankton. Zooplankton also includes larger animals such as jellyfish.

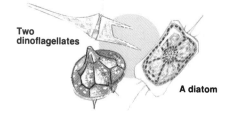

Two dinoflagellates

A diatom

Examples of phytoplankton are pictured above.

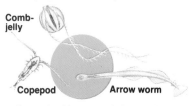

Comb-jelly

Copepod   Arrow worm

Examples of zooplankton are pictured above.

Some planktonic organisms, such as algae, spend their entire lives as plankton. Others, such as fish eggs and larvae, are part of plankton only until they are developed enough to swim off on their own. (*See* NEKTON.)

Plankton is a major source of food for many larger aquatic animals. As such, it is an important part of the aquatic food chain. (*See* FOOD CHAIN.) Many scientists believe that, in the near future, plankton may be cultivated as a major source of food for human beings. *See also* BENTHOS.   A.J.C./R.J.B.

PLANTAIN FAMILY The plantain (plant'-ən) family includes about 265 species of small, herbaceous plants and shrubs. They are dicotyledons (plants with two seed leaves) and are found all over the world. (*See* DICOTYLE-DON; HERBACEOUS PLANT; SHRUB.) The leaves are simple and fleshy and are arranged in opposite pairs. They usually grow in a rosette on the ground. From the middle of the rosette grows a leafless stalk. At the end of this stalk is a spike of tiny green flowers. (*See* INFLOR-ESCENCE; LEAF.)

Common plantain (*Plantago major*) is a well-known plant that is often thought to be a weed when it grows in lawns. Its flowers make tiny nutlike fruits that are a popular food for birds.

The tropical fruit that is called plantain looks like and is related to the banana. (*See* BANANA.) This fruit does not actually come from the plantain family.

A.J.C./M.H.S.

PLANT DISEASE A plant disease (diz ēz') is anything that kills, weakens, or otherwise affects the normal growth of a plant. A great danger of plant diseases is that they will destroy plants that are necessary for people to

The plant diseases barley smut (top) and potato blight (bottom) are pictured.

live. A serious outbreak of a plant disease can cause a famine—widespread lack of food. Famine may result in the starvation and death of hundreds or thousands of people.

The causes of plant diseases can be divided into two major categories: nonliving causes and living causes. Nonliving causes include physical injury, chemical injury, and environmental factors.

Some of the important environmental factors are temperature, water, light, air, and nutrients. If the temperature is very high or low, or changes quickly, it will affect, and possibly kill, the plant. Plants need a certain

Plant diseases can spread rapidly. A blight that periodically attacks locust trees in the United States (left, both pictures) kills large numbers of the trees in a short time.

amount of water to grow. Too little water can cause plants to wilt and die. Too much water, however, can "drown" the roots, killing the plant. Floods or sudden, severe storms can kill plants or help the growth of other diseases that are caused by microorganisms. Air is important to the roots and to photosynthetic tissues. If the air is polluted, it may injure the plant. (*See* PHOTOSYNTHESIS; POLLUTION.) Certain nutrients (nourishing substances) must be in the soil for a plant to grow properly. Some nutrients are needed in fairly large amounts and are called macronutrients (the prefix *macro* means "large"). Micronutrients (the prefix *micro* means "small") are needed in smaller amounts. If certain amounts of these nutrients are not in the soil, plant disease may occur. Many times, farmers and gardeners increase the nutrient content of soil by adding fertilizers. (*See* FERTILIZER.)

The living causes of plant disease include fungi, bacteria, viruses, insects, and nematodes. Most plant diseases are caused by parasitic fungi (plural of *fungus*). (*See* FUNGUS; PARASITE.) When a fungus spore lands on plant tissue, it grows hyphae (rootlike structures) into the plant. These hyphae feed on the plant's cells. Some of the main fungus diseases are blight, mildew, rust, and smut.

There are more than 170 known types of parasitic bacteria that cause diseases in plants. (*See* BACTERIA.) These bacteria are usually carried by insects from plant to plant. They destroy plant cells by digesting plant structures for food.

Viruses cause many plant diseases. (*See* VIRUS.) One of the most harmful viruses is the tobacco mosaic virus, which attacks tobacco and other members of the nightshade family. These viruses may be spread by touch or be carried by insects and other animals.

Some insects cause great damage to plants. Insects can carry harmful microorganisms. They also eat and kill many plants. (*See* INSECT; MICROORGANISM.)

Nematodes are very small worms that sometimes live as parasites on plants. (*See* NEMATODE.) More than one hundred species of nematodes attack plant crops. Although nematodes usually hurt the plant's roots, sometimes they hurt or kill the part of the plant above the ground.

There are many signs of plant disease. These include changes in leaf color; holes in the leaves; enlarged areas on the stem, roots, or leaves; stunted growth (the plant stops growing); falling off or death of parts (flowers, fruits, leaves) of the plant; or the death of the entire plant.

Plant diseases can often be held off by biological or chemical means. (*See* BIOLOGICAL CONTROL; FUNGICIDE; INSECTICIDE; PESTICIDE.) They may also be fought by breeding plants that can hold off some kinds of diseases. *See also* AGRONOMY; BREEDING.

A.J.C./M.H.S.

PLANT KINGDOM The plant kingdom includes all living and extinct (no longer living) plants. The members of the plant kingdom have many cells and are chlorophyll-containing organisms. Other organisms (such as bacteria, fungi, and algae) that were once classified as plants are now placed in separate kingdoms. (*See* CLASSIFICATION OF LIVING ORGANISMS; KINGDOM.)

There are several hundred thousand different species of plants. Unlike animals, most plants stay fixed in one place their entire lives.

How plants differ from animals Plants are different from animals in many ways. Plants are able to make their own food by a process called photosynthesis. In order to make food, plant cells have chlorophyll, a green pigment that "traps" some of the energy from sunlight. (*See* CHLOROPHYLL; PHOTOSYNTHESIS.) Although most plants make more than enough food for themselves, some must depend on other organisms for part or all of their food. (*See* PARASITE; SAPROPHYTE.) However, all animals must depend on other organisms for their food. Some animals eat only plants and are called herbivores. Some animals eat only other animals and are called carnivores. Omnivores are animals that eat both plants and other animals. (*See* CARNIVORE; HERBIVORE; OMNIVORE.)

Most plants stay fixed in one place for their entire lives. Certain parts of the plant can move, but the plant itself does not move. (*See* MOVEMENT OF PLANTS.) Most animals, however, are able to move from one place to another under their own power.

It is possible for the growth of plants to be almost unlimited. Animals, however, are usually limited in size—they cannot grow beyond a certain size.

A plant cell is different from an animal cell. (*See* CELL.) Both the plant cell and animal cell have many similar structures. The plant cell, however, has a thick cell wall surrounding it, while the animal cell has only a cell membrane.

Divisions of plants There are several hundred thousand different species of plants. They are grouped into several divisions (sometimes called phyla.) Members of the division Bryophyta—liverworts, hornworts, and mosses—do not have special conducting tissues (xylem and phloem). They also do not have true roots, stems, or leaves. (*See* BRYOPHYTE.) The division Pterophyta includes ferns, which have conducting tissues, roots, stems, and leaves but do not produce seeds. (*See* PTEROPHYTE.) The division Coniferophyta (conifers) includes the familiar evergreens that produce seeds in cones. They and the other plants that produce seeds that are not completely enclosed in a protective structure are often called gymnosperms. (*See* CONIFER; EVERGREEN; GYMNOSPERM.) The division Anthrophyta includes all flowering plants, often called angiosperms. They produce seeds that are enclosed within a protective structure called a fruit. (*See* ANGIOSPERM; FLOWER; FRUIT.)

The bryophytes, pterophytes, gymnosperms, and angiosperms are the main plant divisions. However, there are other, smaller divisions of plants as well. For example, club mosses and horsetails belong to one small division of plants. Club mosses and horsetails were common prehistoric plants. They grew as tall as modern-day trees. A few species of smaller club mosses and horsetails still exist today. (*See* CLUB MOSS; HORSETAIL.)

Characteristics of different kinds of vascular plants Vascular plants are plants that have special tissue for conducting liquids. (*See* VASCULAR PLANT.) Ferns (pterophytes) are among the simplest of the vascular plants. In prehistoric times, ferns grew as tall as trees. In tropical areas today, some ferns still grow 40 ft. [12 m] tall. However, most ferns do not grow taller than 3.3 ft. [1 m].

The gymnosperms include conifers, cycads, ginkgoes, and gnetales. Most conifers are evergreen trees and shrubs with needle-like leaves. The cycads have large cones and fernlike leaves. The ginkgoes are conifers

with fernlike leaves. All but one species are now extinct. The gnetales are plants with some characteristics of gymnosperms and

Ferns are among the simplest of the vascular plants.

some of angiosperms. Gymnosperms are found throughout the world in almost every type of climate.

The angiosperms—flowering plants—are the most highly evolved, or developed, members of the plant kingdom. Most of the plants in the world today are angiosperms. They show great variety in size, appearance, and ways of life. Most live on land. Some, however, live in fresh water. Some live in salt water. Some live in the air. Some live in hot, dry, desert areas. Some plants live in icy, arctic regions. (*See* AQUATIC PLANT; EPIPHYTE; HALOPHYTE; XEROPHYTE.) Angiosperms are divided into two classes according to the structure of the seed the plant makes: monocotyledons and dicotyledons. Monocotyledons have seeds with one cotyledon. (*See* MONOCOTYLEDON.) Dicotyledons have seeds with two cotyledons. (*See* DICOTYLEDON.)

Structure of a flowering plant Flowering plants have vegetative structures (roots, stems,

Most of the plants in the world today are angiosperms, or flowering plants. At top left is monkshood, which is poisonous. At top right are marigolds, grown not only for their beauty but also to protect nearby plants. Marigolds' roots secrete a chemical that kills nematodes— tiny worms that attack plants. At bottom is part of a garden containing various kinds of angiosperms, carefully arranged.

The tulip (above) is native to Asia and the Mediterranean region. There are about two thousand kinds of this bulbous flowering plant.

leaves) and reproductive structures (flowers, fruits, seeds). The roots hold the plant in the ground and soak up water and minerals from the soil. (See ROOT.) Stems vary greatly in size, appearance, and structure. (See STEM.) Most stems are aerial—they grow above the ground. In general, aerial stems hold up the branches, leaves, and flowers. They also carry food, water, and minerals between the roots and other plant structures. Some stems are subterranean—they grow below the ground. Many underground stems have storage or rootlike structures such as bulbs, corms, and tubers. (See BULB AND CORM; TUBER.) Most stems have buds that make leaves, branches, or flowers. (See BUD.) The bud at the end of a stem is called the terminal bud. It controls the release of plant hormones that regulate growth. (See HORMONE.) Buds along the sides of the stem are called lateral buds. Each lateral bud forms at a place on the stem called a node. Flowers sometimes grow just above the node, in the axil. Many stems have tiny openings called lenticels. The lenticels let gases pass into and out of the stem.

Leaves also show great variety in size and shape. (See LEAF.) Most photosynthesis takes place in the leaves. Most leaves are green because they include large amounts of the pigment (coloring substance) chlorophyll. Some leaves are large and fleshy, storing food and water. Some plants have leaves that have developed into needles, spines, or prickles. Some plants, such as deciduous trees, lose their

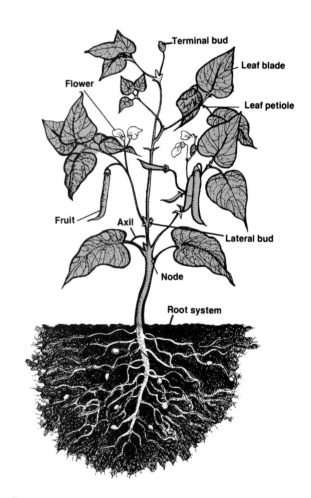

The illustration above shows the structure and parts of a typical flowering plant. Flowering plants have vegetative structures—roots, stems, and leaves—and reproductive structures—flowers, fruits, and seeds.

leaves every year. Other plants, such as evergreens, have leaves year-round. (See DECIDUOUS TREE.)

The flower is the reproductive structure of an angiosperm. Most flowers have four parts: the calyx (sepals), the corolla (petals), the stamens (pollen-producing male structures), and the pistils (ovule-producing female structures). Although some of these parts may be missing, every flower must have at least one stamen or one pistil.

Fertilization occurs when pollen reaches the egg. (*See* FERTILIZATION; POLLINATION.) This takes place in an ovule within the ovary of the pistil. The fertilized egg develops into an embryo. (*See* EMBRYO.) The ovule develops into a seed, and the ovary develops into a fruit. (*See* SEED.) The function of the fruit is to help scatter the seeds of the plant. (*See* DISPERSION

The seeds of some plants, such as this dandelion, are equipped with structures that help them be dispersed by the wind.

OF PLANTS.) It is possible for each normal seed to germinate (sprout) and develop into a new plant.

Plant evolution and adaptation Scientists believe that the first plants were algaelike and lived in the oceans about four billion years ago during the Precambrian time. (*See* EVOLUTION;

PRECAMBRIAN TIME.) The first land plants were probably the primitive psilophytes. (*See* PSILOPHYTE.) These plants probably evolved from the algaelike plants about 400 million years ago during the Paleozoic era. (*See* PALEOZOIC ERA.) By about 340 million years ago, there were forests of club mosses, horsetails, and ferns. By the beginning of the Mesozoic era, about 225 million years ago, when dinosaurs roamed the earth, gymnosperms had become the most widespread of the land plants. By the end of the Mesozoic era, angiosperms had

Long ago, a flower was covered by a thick layer of volcanic ash. In time, the ash hardened into rock, and the flower was preserved as the fossil shown here.

evolved. (*See* MESOZOIC ERA.) By the beginning of the Cenozoic era, about 65 million years ago, angiosperms had spread throughout the world. (*See* CENOZOIC ERA.)

As evolution continued, many plants developed lifestyles or special structures to help them grow and reproduce. Some plants grow, reproduce, and die in one year. (*See* ANNUAL PLANT.) Some plants grow for one year, then reproduce and die in the second year. (*See* BIENNIAL PLANT.) Many plants live for more than two years, usually reproducing every year. (*See* PERENNIAL PLANT.) Some plants have developed structures to protect them from being eaten by animals. In some of these plants, the leaves have been modified (changed) as spines or thorns for protection. In others, the plant has a bad tasting or poisonous fluid in the roots, stems, leaves, flowers, or fruits.

Corn (above left) is raised for food for people and livestock. It is also used in a variety of nonfood products. Peppers (above right) are used primarily to flavor salads and other dishes.

Many plants have evolved special structures to help them get or store food. Bulbs, corms, tubers, fleshy stems, and fleshy leaves are all food-storing structures. Some plants have haustoria, specialized rootlike structures that grow into a host and soak up food and water. (*See* HAUSTORIA.) Some plants have even evolved special structures for catching insects so that the plants can get the minerals they need. (*See* CARNIVOROUS PLANT.) Other plants have developed a lifestyle in which they live symbiotically with other organisms. (*See* SYMBIOSIS.)

Uses of plants Plants are the most important living things on earth. Without plants, there would be no other forms of life. It is believed that plants were the original source of all the oxygen in the earth's early atmosphere. Plants are also the main source of oxygen in the air today. They help balance the carbon dioxide and oxygen levels in the air.

Plants are the source of all food needed by animals. They are vital links in the food chain. (*See* FOOD CHAIN.) Plants are important in practically every cycle in nature—the carbon cycle, the nitrogen cycle, the oxygen cycle, and so forth.

Plants provide many useful nonfood products for people. They provide lumber for construction, fibers for clothing, chemicals for medicines, and hundreds of other substances that have become common parts of everyday life. *See also* BOTANY; ECOLOGY; PLANT DISEASE; REPRODUCTION.　　A.J.C./M.J.C.; M.H.S.

PLAQUE *See* CARIES.

PLASMA (plaz′mə) Plasma is the straw-colored liquid part of the blood that carries the solid parts of blood—red and white cells and platelets. (*See* BLOOD.) Plasma is made of water, salt, protein, and other materials.

Plasma carries food that has been dissolved to all parts of the body. It picks up waste material from body cells and carries it to organs that remove waste from the body. (*See* EXCRETION.)

Plasma contains many proteins that are essential for the proper functioning of the body. (*See* PROTEIN.) One of the proteins found in plasma is fibrinogen. Fibrinogen

Plasma is the part of blood that carries red and white blood cells and platelets. Plasma can be separated from whole blood, frozen, and stored (above) for long periods until it is needed for life-saving transfusions.

helps make it possible for the blood to clot (thicken and lump together) and seal off a wound. If it were not for fibrinogen, a person could bleed to death from the smallest cut. Globulins are another type of protein found in plasma. Globulins are mostly antibodies that help the body's immune system fight disease. (*See* ANTIBODY; IMMUNITY.) A third type of protein found in plasma is albumin. Albumin helps keep the blood pressure and blood volume normal and helps transport certain substances in the blood.

During the 1930s, researchers found that plasma could be separated from whole blood by using a machine called a centrifuge. (*See* CENTRIFUGE.) After plasma has been separated from whole blood, it can be frozen and will keep for a long period of time. Plasma is used in blood transfusions (transferring blood from one person to another person) to restore blood that has been lost due to injury or disease. *See also* BLOOD TRANSFUSION.

W.R.P./J.J.F.; M.H.M.

PLASMA (PHYSICS) Plasma (plaz′mə) is a fourth state of matter. (*See* STATES OF MATTER.) Solids, liquids, and gases are called states of matter. If a solid is heated, it melts and turns into a liquid. At a higher temperature, the liquid boils to form a gas. The fourth state of matter, plasma, is made by heating a gas to above 90,000°F. [50,000°C]. Plasmas can also be made by passing electricity through a gas.

All atoms have small particles called electrons. (*See* ATOM; ELECTRON.) In a plasma, some of the electrons are separated from the atoms. When an atom loses (or gains) an electron, it is called an ion. (*See* IONS AND IONIZATION.) Plasma contains many ions.

Plasmas usually give off light. The light comes mostly from the electrons and the ions

Lightning bolts consist of plasma as the term is used in physics. Plasma is the fourth state of matter, which is produced by heating a gas to an extremely high temperature or passing electricity through it.

coming into contact, or touching. Arc lamps and fluorescent lamps give off light because they contain plasmas. (*See* ELECTRIC LIGHT.) The Van Allen belts around the earth and the corona around the sun are also made of plasmas. (*See* CORONA; VAN ALLEN BELTS.) Plasmas are good carriers of electricity. They are strongly affected by magnetic fields. *See also* MATTER.

M.E./J.T.

PLASMODIUM (plaz mōd′ē əm) Plasmodium is a shapeless mass of protoplasm that has many nuclei (plural of *nucleus*) but lacks a firm cell wall. (*See* CELL.) It moves by oozing

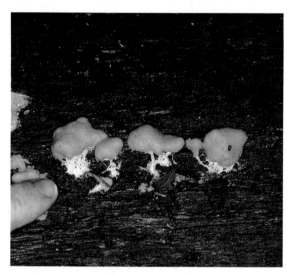

Slime mold (above) is usually in the form of a plasmodium, a formless mass of protoplasm that does not have a firm cell wall. It moves by oozing from one place to another.

from one place to another in what is called ameboid movement. Plasmodium is the normal body form of slime molds and some fungi (plural of *fungus*). (*See* FUNGUS; SLIME MOLD.) *Plasmodium* is also the name of a genus of malaria-causing protozoans. *See also* MALARIA; PROTOZOAN.

A.J.C./C.R.N.

PLASTER OF PARIS Plaster of Paris is a white powder that is a form of calcium sulfate ($CaSO_4 \cdot \frac{1}{2}H_2O$). It is made by removing water from the mineral gypsum ($CaSO_4 \cdot 2H_2O$) when the mineral is heated to 482°F. [250°C]. When water is added to plaster of Paris, it sets in a few minutes to form a hard mass of gypsum. Plaster of Paris sets without any change

of volume. This makes it an ideal material for casts, molds, and pottery. *See also* GYPSUM.

J.J.A./A.D.

PLASTIC (plas′tik) Plastics are synthetic (human-made) materials. Most common plastics belong to a group of chemical compounds called synthetic resins. (*See* RESIN.) Plastics are made of long, chainlike molecules called polymers. (*See* POLYMER.) Some of the polymers used to make plastics are found in nature. For example, celluloid is made by treating cellulose, a naturally occuring polymer, with a mixture of sulfuric and nitric acids. (*See* CELLULOID; CELLULOSE.)

Plastics are easily molded into shapes, usually by applying heat and pressure. Plastic objects have many different uses. In the home, plastic is used in floor tiles, nonstick cooking pans, and heat-proof surfaces in the kitchen. Curtains, carpets, and light fixtures may be made from plastic. Drip-dry shirts, non-iron dresses, and many types of shoes have plastic in them.

Plastics are also very important in industry and medicine. For example, plastic tubes are used in surgery for replacing blood vessels that are no longer working as they should. The plastic used is inert. This means that the body will not have a reaction to the tubing. Few other materials could be used in this way. (*See* PROSTHETICS.)

Types of plastic There are two main groups of plastics: thermoplastics and thermosets. Thermosets are hard and rigid. Thermoplastics are softer and more flexible than thermosets. These two types of plastics act differently when they are heated. Thermosets tend to resist heat. For example, a hot pan from the stove can be placed on top of a thermoset

The development of sturdy plastic films has made it possible to build structures, such as these greenhouses, more cheaply than ever before.

plastic without hurting the plastic. A hot pan, however, would melt most thermoplastics. Thermoplastics soften and melt at fairly low temperatures. Melting does not damage them, however, and they harden again when they are cooled. This process of melting and cooling a thermoplastic can be repeated many times.

Thermosets and thermoplastics are different from each other because their molecules are arranged differently. In thermoplastics, the long chain molecules are mostly separate from each other. There is very little linkage between the chains. This is why thermoplastics are flexible, especially when they are warmed. In thermoset plastics, the long chain molecules are linked together. The linkage of molecules in thermosets makes these materials hard and rigid. When a thermoset is heated, even more linkages form. This is why thermosets do not melt when they are heated. (*See* MOLECULE.)

Most of the well-known plastics are thermoplastics. Besides nylon and polyethylene, they include polystyrene, polyvinyl chloride (PVC),

acrylic, polyacetal, and polytetrafluoroethylene (PTFE). (*See* ACRYLIC; NYLON.) Common thermosetting plastics include Bakelite, epoxy resins, urea-formaldehyde resin, polyurethane, and silicones. (*See* BAKELITE; EPOXY RESIN; SILICONE.)

Some plastics can be either thermosetting or thermoplastic. An example is polyester. Thermoplastic polyester is used in fabrics and to make fiberglass. (*See* FIBERGLASS.)

Making and shaping plastics Plastics are made by a process called polymerization. In polymerization, small molecules called monomers are linked together to make the long chainlike molecules called polymers. For polymerization to happen, a catalyst is usually needed to speed the polymers in linking up. (*See* CATALYST.)

In order to make plastic articles, the plastic has to be shaped. The most common way of shaping plastic is by molding it. Different processes are used for thermosets and thermoplastics. Objects made of thermoset plastic are produced by compression molding. In this process, plastic pellets are placed in the bottom half of a hot mold. The top half of the mold is moved down on top of the bottom half with a great deal of pressure. This melts the plastic, causing it to flow into the shape of the mold. Under these conditions of high pressure and temperature, the molecules link up, and the plastic sets, or molds.

Thermoplastics are much easier to shape than thermosets. This is because thermoplastics can be kept molten (melted) for a long time. There are several different methods of molding thermoplastics. A very common method is called injection molding. Plastic pellets are melted in a heated chamber. A piston then forces the molten plastic through a nozzle into a mold that is kept cool. The plastic cools and sets in the shape of the mold. The mold then opens automatically, and the object is taken out of the mold.

Another method is called blow molding. Molten thermoplastic is placed inside a mold. The mold is kept cool by water. Air is then blown into the plastic to force it into the right shape. This method is used for making plastic bottles and other hollow articles.

Another common method for shaping thermoplastic is called extrusion. (*See* EXTRUSION.) In this method, molten plastic is forced through a hole in the shape of the object to be made. For example, a circular hole is used for making rods and a slit for making films. Synthetic fibers are made this way. Molten plastic is forced through very tiny holes in a special device called a spinneret. This method is used for nylon and polyester. (*See* FIBER.)

The heat-resistant countertops used in kitchens are made by a different process called laminating. Layers of cloth or paper are soaked in a resin such as urea-formaldehyde. The resin makes the structure strong and rigid. The layers are then clamped in a press and heated to set the resin. This forms the thick plastic countertop.

Plastics and the environment Even though plastics have become a "wonder material," they pose great problems for the environment. For example, plastics are made from a nonrenewable natural resource—petroleum. (*See* NATURAL RESOURCE; PETROLEUM.) The manufacture of plastics releases poisons into the air and creates hazardous waste. (*See* WASTE DISPOSAL.) These liquid and solid wastes can cause cancer in humans and other animals if they are poorly disposed of and leak into the soil or water. Plastic products also make up close to one-fifth of the solid waste in the United States. Because they do not biodegrade (break down), they take up valuable space in landfills and other disposal sites forever. (*See* BIODEGRADABILITY.) Also, improperly discarded plastic materials can cause damage to many organisms. For example, rings that hold cans together, fishing lines, and fishing nets can strangle sea animals. Sea turtles can choke on plastic bags they mistake for jellyfish.

Some manufacturers claim their plastic grocery and trash bags are biodegradable. However, the process of making these bags involves bonding small plastic pieces together with cornstarch. (*See* STARCH.) The cornstarch decomposes, but the plastic pieces do not. These claims may cause harm if they lead people away from researching how plastics can be recycled. *See also* RECYCLING.

C.C; M.E./J.M.; J.E.P.

PLASTIC SURGERY (plas'tik sərj'ə rē) Plastic surgery is the surgical repair or rebuilding of body tissues. (*See* SURGERY.) Plastic surgeons treat physical defects (something that is wrong with the body) that existed when a person was born (congenital defects) or defects that were caused by injury or disease. Often, a natural body part does not work as it should. In such cases, the surgeon does reconstructive plastic surgery to improve the body part's function and appearance. This often requires grafting. In grafting, skin, muscle, bone, or cartilage is transplanted from a healthy part of the body to the part that is hurt or damaged. Sometimes, reconstructive surgery involves reattaching severed limbs, rebuilding damaged tissues, or restoring damaged blood vessels and nerves.

People who want to make their appearance better sometimes have cosmetic plastic surgery. The most common types of cosmetic surgery are face-lifts to take away wrinkles from the face and neck and rhinoplasties to change the shape of the nose. *See also* IMPLANTATION; TRANSPLANTATION.

A.J.C./J.J.F.; M.H.M.

PLATELET (plāt′lət) Platelets are tiny, colorless disks found in blood plasma that help blood clot. When a person receives a cut, clotting is the mechanism that prevents excessive blood loss, which may cause death. Platelets measure about 0.00008 to 0.00016 in. [0.002 to 0.004 mm] in diameter. They are produced by bone marrow. (*See* BLOOD; MARROW; PLASMA.) Platelets live for about eight days. They cannot move on their own and are carried by the bloodstream.

When a blood vessel is cut, platelets stick to the damaged edges and to each other. They form a temporary seal over the injury. As the platelets pile up, they release a chemical that combines with other substances in plasma. This reaction produces the chemical called thromboplastin. Thromboplastin changes a blood chemical called prothrombin into thrombin. Thrombin acts on another blood chemical called fibrinogen. Thrombin changes fibrinogen so that it takes the form of threads. The threads form a permanent seal called a clot that stops the escape of blood through the wound.

Platelets occur only in mammals. (*See* MAMMAL.) In other vertebrates (organisms with a backbone) and some invertebrates, cells called thrombocytes perform a similar function. P.Q.F./J.E.P.

PLATE TECTONICS (plāt tek tän′iks) Plate tectonics is the theory that the earth's lithosphere (solid portion) consists of plates (big, movable, flat pieces of rock). Some of these plates include continents, while others include both continents and oceans. According to this theory, the movement and interaction of these plates causes continental drift (the slow movement of the continents), volcanoes, mountain building, and earthquakes. (*See* CONTINENTAL DRIFT.)

The San Andreas Fault in California is where the North American plate meets the Pacific plate. The area around this fault is very likely to have earthquakes. Earthquakes are also likely to occur along faults in other parts of the world. Volcanoes also are likely to occur along the edges of faults. (*See* EARTHQUAKE; FAULT; SAN ANDREAS FAULT; VOLCANO.)

Convection currents are forces beneath the earth's crust that carry molten (melted) material from the inside of the earth to the surface. Convection currents have played a part in the formation of the Mid-Atlantic ridge. Along this ridge, new rock is always being formed from the molten material. The new rock forces the two plates that meet at

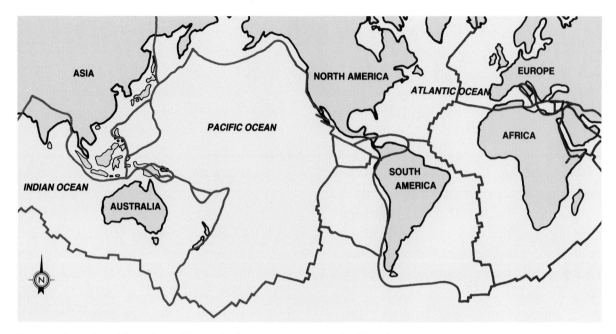

The map shows in red the edges of the plates that make up the earth's lithosphere.

this ridge to spread apart. Scientists think that this tectonic activity is slowly moving the American continents away from Europe and Africa.

Tectonic activity also explains how mountain ranges have formed. (*See* MOUNTAIN.) For example, millions of years ago, the plate carrying the Indian peninsula crashed into the Asian plate. This caused the Himalayas to rise up.

The plate tectonic theory provides an explanation for many of the unusual geological events that have happened during the last several billion years. *See also* EARTH.

J.M.C./W.R.S.

PLATINUM (plat′nəm) Platinum (Pt) is a rare, silvery metallic element. (*See* ELEMENT.) Platinum is found as grains or nuggets in igneous rocks. (*See* ROCK.) It is a hard metal and is resistant to (not hurt by) heat and many chemicals. For these reasons, it is used to make surgical instruments, chemical equipment, and electrodes. (*See* ELECTRODE.) It is also easily shaped into a new form. Platinum is used in a number of different alloys. An alloy is a mixture of different metals. (*See* ALLOY.) Alloys of platinum and silver are used in dentistry. Alloys of platinum with the metal iridium are used for making electrical parts and bearings. Platinum's resistance to heat allows it to be used as a coating in nose cones of missiles and in fuel nozzles for jet engines. Platinum is used to make fine jewelry. It is also an important catalyst in many chemical reactions. A catalyst is a substance that speeds up a chemical reaction. (*See* CATALYST.)

Platinum's atomic number is 78, and its atomic weight is 195.09. Platinum melts at 3,222°F. [1,772°C] and boils at about 6,900°F. [3,800°C]. Its relative density is 21.5. *See also* RELATIVE DENSITY.   M.E./J.R.W.

PLATYHELMINTHES (plat′ i hel minth′ēz) Platyhelminthes is a phylum of animals that includes a large class of free-living flatworms and two classes of parasitic flatworms, the flukes and the tapeworms. (*See* PARASITE; TAPEWORM.) These invertebrate animals have soft, flat bodies. They have no true skeleton, respiratory system, or circulatory system. The platyhelminths have primitive nervous and excretory (waste-removal) systems. Most have digestive systems with a single opening. The most common nonparasitic flatworms are the freshwater planarians. *See also* INVERTEBRATE; SCHISTOSOMIASIS; WORM. S.R.G./C.S.H.

PLATYPUS (plat′i pəs) The platypus, or duckbill (*Ornithorhynchus anatinus*), is a primitive mammal found in parts of Australia and the island of Tasmania. (*See* MAMMAL.) The animal is often called a duckbill because of its ducklike bill. The platypus uses its bill to hunt for shellfish, worms, and various insects on the bottom of streams. Adult platypuses have no teeth. Instead, they use the horny plates in their upper and lower jaws to chew food.

The platypus (above) uses its unique, ducklike bill to hunt for shellfish, worms, and aquatic insects. The platypus is found in parts of Australia and on the island of Tasmania.

The platypus is about 2 ft. [61 cm] long, not including the tail. The tail, which is 6 in. [15 cm] long, is shaped like a paddle. It helps the animal swim.

Although the platypus lays eggs instead of bearing its young alive, it is a mammal. It is classified in the order Monotremata. (*See* MONOTREME.) Like other mammals, the platypus nurses its young—that is, feeds them with milk from the mother's breast. The female usually lays from one to three eggs. When they are hatched, she uses her tail to hold the young close to her body while nursing them.

Platypuses were once killed in great numbers for their thick, soft fur. Hunting platypuses is now against the law in Australia and Tasmania, where the animals live.

J.J.A./J.J.M.

PLEISTOCENE EPOCH (plī′stə sēn ep′ək) The Pleistocene epoch is the division of the Quaternary period in the earth's history that began 2 million years ago and ended about 10,000 years ago. Modern humans emerged during the Pleistocene epoch.

The Pleistocene epoch was marked by several ice ages—periods of time when much of the earth was covered with ice. (*See* ICE

Some large mammals that lived during the Pleistocene epoch are shown above: (1) mammoth; (2) Irish elk; (3) woolly rhinoceros; (4) giant sloth; (5) giant armadillo; and (6) saber-toothed cat.

AGE.) During the ice ages, there was less water in the oceans than there is now because of the large amount of frozen water in the glaciers (large bodies of ice). Land bridges (bridges formed by land over a body of water), such as the Bering Strait, were uncovered. This may have given animals and people the chance to move from the eastern hemisphere into the western hemisphere. When the glaciers melted, the landscape of the northern land areas was changed. (*See* GLACIATION; GLACIER.)

Most modern mammals appeared during the Pleistocene. Toward the end of this epoch, huge mammals such as the mammoths, mastodons, and woolly rhinoceroses became extinct (no longer existed). (*See* EXTINCTION; MAMMOTH; MASTODON.) The reason for the extinction of these large mammals has not yet been determined. *See also* EVOLUTION; GEOLOGICAL TIME SCALE; QUATERNARY PERIOD.

J.M.C./W.R.S.

PLIMSOLL LINE   The Plimsoll (plim′səl) line is a mark on the side of a ship that shows how low in the water the ship can safely sit when it is fully loaded. If the Plimsoll line is below the water level, the ship is too full. A ship that is too full can sink in stormy seas.

The Plimsoll line is named after the British politician Samuel Plimsoll. Plimsoll helped improve the laws for ship safety. A Plimsoll line is now necessary by law on ships of all nations. It is sometimes called the International Load Line.   J.M.C./R.W.L.

PLIOCENE EPOCH (plī′ə sēn′ ep′ək) The Pliocene epoch, the last division of the Tertiary period in the earth's history, began about 7 million years ago and lasted about 5 million years. The Pliocene is the shortest epoch of the Tertiary period. (*See* TERTIARY PERIOD.)

The Pliocene epoch was cooler and drier than the previous epochs. Pliocene mammals began to grow to a larger size. There were many species of camels and horses that were bigger than today's species. Mastodons (elephantlike mammals) that could live in the new environment began to evolve. Primates were also evolving rapidly. (*See* PRIMATE.) The rhinoceroses of North America became extinct (no longer existed). (*See* EXTINCTION.) Pliocene sea life was quite similar to that of today. During the Pliocene epoch, the mountain ranges known as the Alps and the Himalayas were rising. *See also* GEOLOGICAL TIME SCALE.   J.M.C./W.R.S.

PLOVER (pləv′ər) A plover is a bird that belongs to the family Charadriidae. It has a short, straight bill; a short tail; and long, pointed wings. Many plovers are shorebirds.

A blacksmith plover of Africa is pictured.

They are most often seen walking along the shoreline, feeding on insects and small water animals. Other plovers feed in grasslands and meadows some distance from bodies of water.

There are twelve species of plovers in North America. One of the most common plovers is the killdeer. It grows to about 8 in. [20 cm] long. Killdeer have brown wings, white bellies, and two black bands around their necks. All plovers are strong fliers. The American golden plover, a bird about the size of a robin, spends the summer in the arctic but flies to southern South America for the winter. This is one of the longest bird migrations known. *See also* BIRD; MIGRATION.   S.R.G./L.L.S.

PLUM   The plum is a fruit-bearing tree belonging to the rose family, Rosaceae. (*See* ROSE FAMILY.) Its fruit, which can be as large as a peach, is round or oval and contains a stonelike seed. The thin skin may be purple, blue, red, yellow, or green. The flesh of the plum can be eaten fresh. The plum tree, which grows in temperate regions around the world,

The fruit of plum trees is a popular food. Dried plums are called prunes. In the United States, most plums and prunes are grown in California.

can be low and shrubby or grow to 30 ft. [9 m] high.

Almost two thousand varieties of plum are known. The five most common plums are the European plum, the Japanese plum, the American plum, the damson plum, and the ornamental plum. Some of these varieties are used to make jellies, jams, and plum butter. Dried plums are known as prunes. Prunes have a high sugar content.

In the United States, most plums and prunes are grown in California. Oregon, Washington, Idaho, and Michigan are other states where plums are grown for market.

W.R.P./F.W.S.

PLUTO (plü′tō) Pluto is the planet next to Neptune. It is the farthest planet from the sun. (*See* PLANET.) Percival Lowell, an American astronomer, believed there was a planet beyond Neptune. He based his belief on Neptune's unusual orbit. In 1930, Pluto was discovered by Clyde Tombaugh, an assistant to Lowell. (*See* LOWELL, PERCIVAL; TOMBAUGH, CLYDE WILLIAM.) Pluto cannot be seen without a strong telescope.

Pluto is the smallest planet. Pluto's diameter is between 1,500 and 1,800 mi. [2,400 and 2,900 km]. Pluto is, on average, about 3.66 billion mi. [5.89 billion km] from the sun. Pluto takes a little more than 248 years to make a full orbit around the sun. For about 20 years every 248 years, Pluto's orbit is inside Neptune's. Most recently, this period began in 1976. Pluto will again be the most distant planet in 1999.

Very little is known about the surface of Pluto. Its tiny size and great distance from the earth make Pluto the most difficult planet for astronomers to study. Pluto consists largely of gases. Scientists believe that the average tem-

Pluto, the smallest planet, was not discovered until 1930. Because Pluto is so small and so far from earth, little is known about this planet's surface.

perature of Pluto is near absolute zero, which is -459.67°F. [-273.15°C]. This low temperature would cause most of the gases on Pluto to be frozen or at least liquefied.

Until 1978, Pluto was thought to have no natural satellites. However, on June 22, 1978, James W. Christy, an American astronomer, discovered that Pluto has a moon. Christy named the moon Charon. Charon has a diameter of 500 to 600 mi. [800 to 965 km]. It orbits Pluto every 6.4 earth-days, the same time it takes Pluto to make a complete spin on its axis. This type of synchronized (happening at the same time) movement does not happen anywhere else in the solar system. Charon is about 12,000 mi. [19,300 km] from Pluto.

J.M.C./C.R.

PLUTONIUM (plü tō′nē əm) Plutonium (Pu) is a radioactive metallic element. (*See* ELEMENT; RADIOACTIVITY.) Plutonium is the only transuranic element that occurs naturally. (*See* TRANSURANIC ELEMENT.) Before this fact was discovered, a team of American scientists headed by Edwin MacMillan made the element artificially in 1940.

Fifteen isotopes of plutonium have been discovered. (*See* ISOTOPE.) The longest-lasting plutonium isotope is plutonium-239. It takes 24,400 years for half of a given amount of this isotope to decay. (*See* HALF-LIFE.) Plutonium is used as a fuel in some nuclear reactors as well as in nuclear weapons. (*See* NUCLEAR ENERGY; NUCLEAR WEAPONS.) Plutonium-238 was used as a power source for equipment placed on the moon during the Apollo missions.

Plutonium isotopes are extremely poisonous and radioactive. Therefore, disposal of waste products from nuclear reactors and nuclear weapons that use plutonium poses grave problems.

Plutonium's atomic number is 94. It melts at 1,186°F. [641°C] and boils at 5,850°F. [3,232°C]. Its relative density is 19.8. *See also* RELATIVE DENSITY.

M.E./J.R.W.

PNEUMATICS (nü mat′iks) Pneumatics is the branch of mechanics that deals with the

The pneumatic wrench, or bolt tightener, at left is an example of the many tools that work with compressed air.

behavior of compressed gases. In the seventeenth century, the Italian scientist Evangelista Torricelli studied the effects of atmospheric pressure. As a result of Torricelli's work, practical air pumps that could compress air were built. Modern pneumatic devices that work with compressed air include riveting hammers, jackhammers, sandblasting equipment, auto garage tools, and dental drills. Compressed air is also used in some vehicle braking systems and to fill tires. *See also* BRAKE; GAS; MECHANICS. W.R.P./J.T.

PNEUMONIA (nū̇ mō′nyə) Pneumonia is a lung disease that is usually caused by pathogens such as bacteria or viruses. (*See* PATHOGEN.) It may also be caused by exposure to radiation, such as X rays, or by breathing in chemical fumes or powders. Pneumonia causes the alveoli (air sacs) of the lungs to become irritated. (*See* LUNG.) When this happens, white blood cells enter the alveoli to fight the infection. The symptoms of pneumonia include chills, fever, chest pain, coughing, and difficulty in breathing. Frequently, a person with pneumonia coughs up rust-colored phlegm—

mucus that contains blood from the irritated lung tissues. The symptoms usually last for a week to ten days until the body's immune system gets the infection under control. (*See* IMMUNITY.) Antibiotics have greatly reduced the number of deaths due to pneumonia. (*See* ANTIBIOTIC.)

Pneumonia is most commonly caused by bacteria called *Streptococcus pneumoniae,* also called pneumococci. (*See* BACTERIA.) Pneumococci are present in the bodies of many healthy persons, but the immune system usually can keep such bacteria under control. If the body becomes weakened because of surgery, exhaustion, or illness, the pneumococci can quickly overcome the body's defenses and cause pneumonia. Another bacterium (singular of *bacteria*), called *Mycoplasma pneumoniae,* also causes pneumonia. The body develops an immunity to this bacterium, so it does not usually affect a person more than once.

Pneumonia is a serious disease that should always be treated by a doctor. The patient should get plenty of rest, fluids, and fresh air. In addition, he or she should avoid contact with other people.

Viral and bacterial pneumonia are very contagious (catching). The pathogens become airborne when a person who has pneumonia coughs, sneezes, or spits. As a result, pneumonia can quickly become epidemic. *See also* DISEASE; EPIDEMIC; INFECTION; VIRUS. A.J.C./J.J.F.

POISON (pȯiz′ən) A poison is a substance that causes irritation, injury, sickness, and possibly death. The study of poisons is called toxicology.

Corrosive poisons—poisons that slowly eat away at something—kill living tissue that they touch. A person who swallows this type of poison may destroy the lining of the mouth or throat. Lye (sodium hydroxide) is an example of a corrosive poison. (*See* CORROSION; LYE.)

Irritant poisons cause swelling and soreness of the mucous membranes, such as in the nose, stomach, and intestines. (*See* MUCOUS MEMBRANE.) Irritant poisons may also damage nerves. (*See* NERVOUS SYSTEM.)

Systemic poisons attack the nervous system and other important organs, such as the liver and heart. For example, strychnine damages the nervous system, causing convulsions (sudden, uncontrolled muscle movements) and making it difficult for a person to swallow. (*See* CONVULSION.) Many barbiturates, taken in large doses, are also systemic poisons. (*See* BARBITURATE.)

Poisonous gases make it hard for a person to breathe and can sometimes cause death. Some gases irritate the eyes, nose, or skin. Carbon monoxide is a particularly dangerous poisonous gas because it has no odor and so is difficult to detect. (*See* CARBON MONOXIDE.) Carbon monoxide can cause a person to lose consciousness and die.

Food poisoning can come from eating certain chemicals or organisms and their poisons. For example, chemicals such as insecticides can cause food poisoning. When organisms make a poison, the poison is called a toxin. Botulism is poisoning caused by a toxin that certain bacteria make. Botulism can cause paralysis and death. (*See* BOTULISM; FOOD POISONING; TOXIN.)

All cases of poisonings are serious medical emergencies. A physician or poison control center should always be consulted as soon as possible when poisoning is suspected. There are many treatments for poisoning. Each is effective for specific types of poisons. (*See* FIRST AID.) Treatment sometimes includes giving an antidote to the victim. An antidote blocks or weakens the effects of the poison. Some antidotes, such as ipecac syrup, cause a person to vomit. This rids the stomach of the poison. However, if a person has swallowed a corrosive poison, such as lye, vomiting will cause additional damage to the lining of the esophagus, throat, and mouth. In such cases, patients are sometimes advised to eat food that will absorb the poison.

The United States has over one hundred regional poison control centers. Trained specialists at poison control centers answer emergency calls twenty-four hours a day. Most phone books list emergency phone numbers for the nearest poison control center.

The strongest poisons are not usually found in the home or other everyday surroundings. However, over 92 percent of the over 2 million poisonings each year occur at home. The misuse of common household substances, such as alcoholic beverages, cleaning products, cough and cold remedies, cosmetics, prescription medicines, and vitamins cause many poisonings. *See also* CHEMICALS, HOUSEHOLD.

J.J.A.; C.C./J.J.F.; M.H.M.; J.E.P.